GRAY HENRY

SUSANNAH MARRIOTT

BEADS
OF FAITH

GRAY HENRY

SUSANNAH MARRIOTT

BEADS
OF FAITH

CARROLL & BROWN PUBLISHERS LIMITED

First published in the UK in 2002 by
Carroll & Brown Publishers
20 Lonsdale Road, Queen's Park
London NW6 6RD

Editor Anna Amari-Parker
Art Editor Gilda Pacitti

Text copyright © Gray Henry and Susannah Marriott 2002
Selected images © Gray Henry 2002
Illustrations and compilation copyright
© Carroll & Brown Publishers Limited 2002

A CIP catalogue record for this book is available from the British Library
ISBN 1-903258-47-2

Reproduced by RALI, Bilbao, Spain
Printed by Ajanta, New Delhi, India

CONTENTS

Introduction 6

THE UNIVERSAL ROSARY
Sacred Beads..10
Entering Within...14
Calling Out a Holy Name 16

CATHOLIC ROSARIES
The Roman Catholic Prayer Tradition 20
Different Types of Catholic Rosaries 22
Praying with the Rosary...
    Starting to Pray 26
    The Mysteries 28
    Key Prayers 30

ORTHODOX ROSARIES
Prayer Rites in the Orthodox Church 34
The Silent Orthodox Prayer Rope 38
Praying with the Prayer Rope...
    The Jesus Prayer 40
The Anglican Prayer Bead Rope 42
Celtic Christian Prayer 44

THE JEWISH TEFILLIN
Understanding the Jewish *Tefillin* 48
Obeying God's Commandments 50
Inside the *Tefillin*...54
Praying with the *Tefillin*...
    Binding the Words of God................................56

HINDU MALAS
Liberating the Soul 60
The Sacred Associations of the Hindu *Mala*............62
Mantra Yoga 64
Japa Yoga...
    Om 68
    Reciting Holy Names 70

BUDDHIST MALAS
Living and Chanting with Prayer Beads 74
Praying with the Buddhist *Mala* 78
The Lotus Mantra...
    Om Mani Padme Hum 82
The Jain *Mala* 84

THE MUSLIM TASBIH
Glorifying God...88
The *Tasbih* 90
Praying with the *Tasbih*...
    Reciting God's 99 Names 92
Sufi Mysticism 94
Praying with the *Tasbih*...
    The Sufi Way 96

NATIVE AMERICAN BEADS
Dancing with the Spirit World 100
Sacred Beading 102

AMULETS AND MEDITATION
Worry Beads..106
Adapting Traditions 108

Index 110
Acknowledgements...112

INTRODUCTION

The world's great religions use the counting of beads as a form of prayer. Rosaries are not just a sacrament, but a most important means of grace. Around the globe, Hindus, Buddhists, Muslims, Orthodox and Catholic Christians pass rosary beads or knots through their fingers as they praise God, repeating sacred names or *mantras*. Devout Jews profess holy words on 'threads' alone. In all faiths, the repetition of devotional formulae on rosaries acts as an anchor with which to focus thoughts and still the mind, helping devotees to transcend the temporal world and to reside in the sacred present. Retreating within, into God's presence, helps one to re-establish one's innate Divinity.

GIFTS FROM GOD
In many traditions, strings of prayer beads reputedly have miraculous origins. Catholics tell of the Virgin Mary revealing the rosary to St Dominic (1170–1221 CE) in the early 13th century, bidding him teach it to the faithful and, in the last two centuries, this was reinforced by reappearances of the Blessed Virgin at Lourdes, France, and Fatima, Portugal. In Tibet, ancient *dzi*, or Buddha-eye, beads have been found in tilled fields, their origins obscure but considered sanctified. Tiny seed beads used in Native American beadwork are thought to be gifts sent by the Great Spirit, while the same auspicious materials – crystal, amber, rosewood, olive pits – are revered and incorporated in rosaries universally. The holy basil shrub known as *tulsi*, which is used in sacred Hindu *mala* beads, for instance, is said in Greece to have grown on Christ's grave.

DIVINE WORDS
Prayers repeated upon sanctified beads are intensified by the spiritual power conferred on them by being uttered in sacred and ancient languages that have been Divinely revealed, such as Sanskrit, Chinese, Arabic or in

liturgical Greek or Latin. The centuries-old devotion of saints and illuminated individuals has instilled a holiness in the words of prayers that, through their repetition, can open the gates to the Divine realm. Reciting the Sanskrit word *Om*, for example, is thought to bring the believer into resonance with every part of the universe. The aims of rosary prayers are remarkably similar across cultures: impressing the words of God upon the heart helps one be able to "pray without ceasing", so that every act is carried out with an awareness of God. This is the purpose of the Sioux and Cheyenne tribes, the Orthodox monk and the Sufi seeker alike. Many faiths also resolve to send out blessings and love to every living being by means of invocatory prayer reinforced by beads, whether these be in the Buddhist tradition of the loving-kindness meditation or the prayer ceremonies involving sacred beaded objects of the Crow and Huichol Native American Indians.

A LIVING TRADITION

Beads of Faith profiles the rosary prayer traditions of all the world's great religions, looking at the history and timeless rituals surrounding the strings of beads and the words repeated while using them.

You will find a selection of glorious colour photographs depicting rosary beads of all types: from chunks of Tibetan amber to exquisitely carved Italian coral; from fragrant beads pressed from rose petals to silken Turkish tassels. Accompanying the analysis of each faith tradition is at least one simple *mantra* or prayer that you might like to experience. Followers of all faiths – or none – can but gain in spiritual insight through honouring devotions, such as the profound Jesus Prayer of the Christian Orthodox tradition, the *Om* chant of the Hindu faithful, or the heart-opening Muslim prayer – the simple repetition of the name of God 99 times.

We hope these sublime words and beautiful beads may inspire you.

V. Gray Henry   Susannah Marriott

THE
UNIVERSAL
ROSARY

THE USE OF PRAYER BEADS IS NOT A practice recently invented or introduced, but is archetypal in nature, and common to every great faith tradition. According to all major world religions, life's sojourn on earth is for the perfection of the soul. Historically, people the world over have enjoyed the assistance of a rosary, or prayer beads, usually accompanied by the invocation of a Divine name. Across religions, this powerful rite is believed to help guide the believer towards the path of self-realisation and virtue. All sacred traditions hold that human beings are innately Divine. Religion helps to recover this true status, and the use of the rosary across different faiths has this goal as its particular focus.

SACRED BEADS

A rosary is a string of beads or knots used both to activate the memory and as a device to count recitations of prayers, or repetitions of the name or attributes of the Divinity. Although the number, grouping and material of the beads vary from tradition to tradition, many of the ideas they embody are universal. In whichever faith they are used, the very act of pausing on a bead brings you back to the centre of where you are and *who* you are. The etymology of the word "bead" helps to clarify and reinforce the meaning and transcendental function of prayer beads, deriving as it does both from the Sanskrit *buddh*, which refers to self-realisation – the Buddha being the Enlightened One – and from the Saxon verb *bidden*, "to pray".

GARDEN OF PRAYER

The derivation of the word "rose" signals a common meeting point across cultures, sharing as it does an Indo-European root with the Persian *gul*. *Gulistan* means "rose garden", as does the Latin *rosarium*, from which "rosary" derives. This garden is, of course, associated with the garden of Eden or Paradise. "Paradise" comes from the Persian *firdaus* and, etymologically, the Arabic words *jenna* (paradise) and *janaina* (garden) share the same linguistic root.

A secluded rose garden, like a quiet cloister, is a contemplative place for the soul's repose and recreation – somewhere for self-cultivation, prayer and meditation. Just as the earthly garden has long been considered the counterpart or Divine emanation of the celestial garden, so the human heart became the traditional focus for the Kingdom of Heaven within. Persian carpets displaying *gul* medallions, or "roses", were designed to help devotees feel that they were surrounded by or were sitting in a garden setting. The recurrence of this type of repetitive woven motif was even reputed to induce a natural state of contemplation.

This intriguing connection is further evident in the Arabic word for "rosary", *wardiya*, which has at its root the letters w-r-d, *ward* meaning "rose".

From the 15th century onwards, when the rose became a symbol for the Blessed Virgin herself, visual depictions of the Virgin and child in horticultural settings, such as *The Madonna of the Garden* by Stefano da Verona, featured frequently in religious art.

In the ancient Semitic language, from which derives Hebrew, Arabic and even Aramaic, the language spoken by Christ, the linguistic root of *ward* means "watering-place". Other definitions include "to blossom", "bloom into", "to enter", "arrive" or "travel to", all words which richly resonate the importance of prayer in taking the believer on an inward journey to a higher state of awareness through language and imagery that links the garden with self-cultivation.

Mala, the Buddhist and Hindu word for prayer beads, also signifies a garland of flowers. One of the meanings of *japamala*, invocatory prayers said daily on a rosary, is "rose chaplet", perhaps because prayer beads were originally made from actual petals. Catholic rosaries, too, were pressed from rose-petal paste and this medieval tradition survives to the present day. Only rose petals yield sufficient oil to allow the making and shaping of such beads.

THE SACRED CIRCLE
The garland of flowers and the circlet of beads both draw upon the power of the never-ending circle found in the circular cycle of prayers common to diverse faith traditions. From Celtic Christians to Native Americans, people of different religions and from different historical periods have honoured circles as enclosed places of mystical protection, symbolically bringing people together to ward off the advent of danger. St Augustine (354–430 CE) said, "God is a circle, whose centre is everywhere." The circle also echoes the cyclical flow of nature and of the human seasons: birth, life, death and rebirth. There are other historical connections as well: in the Middle Ages, *bedesmen* were specifically employed in England to pray for the souls of the deceased, who were buried holding a rosary, these having, and to this day continuing to have, associations with death and salvation.

Brother René Richee makes handmade rose-petal rosary beads as part of his daily routine at the Monastery of Gethsemane in Bardstown, Kentucky, USA. The petals are gathered from the garden, ground into a paste, then rolled by hand into tiny balls and individually dried on a needle-stick until they shrink and harden. Strung together, they form a rosary which retains the fragrance of roses for up to 50 years.

A gold Thai Buddha statue adorned with a garland of flowers serves as a reminder of Buddhism's wordless flower sermon. On this occasion, Siddhartha Gautama, the Buddha, chose to preach silently by simply holding up a flower. This meditative silence reflects the focused quiet of the enclosed rose garden in other religions, which is outside place and beyond time.

ENTERING WITHIN

If the rose garden symbolises the Kingdom of Heaven, our nearest doorway to it is through the human heart. "Know thyself, [and] the Kingdom of Heaven is within" teach both Christianity and Islam.

Within this interior garden, with its central fountain which recalls the garden of Eden's fount of immortality, the gardener or pilgrim effectively aims to perfect the heart as an oratory for continual prayer and praise of God. St Augustine (354–430 CE) preached that the afterlife will be dedicated to praising God and that there is no time like the present within which to prepare: "None can become fit for the future life who hath not practised himself for it now".

FINDING STILLNESS

In Frances Hodgson Burnett's classic children's book, the sacred, or rather *The Secret Garden* (1911), one of the children, an ailing lad, first sets foot inside the garden to proclaim, "I shall live forever" and gradually begins to recover his health. Similarly for the faithful across religions, achieving immortality beyond time and space is the ultimate aim of using prayer beads during worship.

By reciting prayers or holy names with the aid of a rosary, the world, as limited by reason, thinking and imposed belief systems, gets left behind. The circlet of prayer beads creates a protective shield which excludes the ceaseless movement of the external, anchors the physical to a repetitive touch pattern, stills the machinations of the perturbed mind and enhances the solitary state required for effective prayer.

As the mind places sacred words into a humble and empty heart with each bead, one enters the realm of pure being to witness God's presence. If you are agitated with concern, simply utter a Divine name with each bead: plunge your consciousness into the quiet of the heart's garden and remain there as a motionless flame until you come to reside in total connectedness with all that is.

"It is in the inward man that truth dwells."
ST AUGUSTINE
(354–430 CE)

"Peace comes from within. Do not seek it without."
THE BUDDHA
(563–483 BCE)

CALLING OUT A HOLY NAME

I n order to progress towards self-knowledge and a Divine stillness within, the use of a rosary, or prayer beads has, for the most part, been accompanied by invocations of a Divine name. The power of a sacred name can imbue the utterer with the sanctity of the Named, so the invocation of God's name, or of one of His attributes, has long served as an established methodology for spiritual realisation.

NAMING THE DIVINE

From the Persian word *wirds* comes the English "word", the Gothic *waurd* and, most interestingly, the Lithuanian *vardus*, which means "name". This suggests that the word for something is essentially its *name*. The early medieval Spanish Muslim saint Ibn Arabi (1165–1240 CE) revealingly refers to God's all-pervading presence by using a metaphor of revelation: "His prophet is He, and His sending is He, and His Word is He. He sent Himself, with Himself, to Himself."

Essentially, there is no difference between the sender, what is sent, the sending and the recipient. God's word, or *logos*, or name *is* God, or His shadow, at the very least.

A name of God, Divinely revealed, legitimately bestowed by a proper spiritual authority and frequently invoked, reconsecrates the altar of the temple, or the heart of the believer, and functions in a direct way to reanimate the Holy Spirit or latent Divine breath within.

When the finite and temporal human heart is rhythmically impressed with a Divine name, which by its very nature participates in the infinite and the eternal, the heart cannot resist and invariably recalls its theomorphic essence.

> *"In the beginning was the Word, and the Word was with God, and the Word was God."*
>
> ST JOHN (1:1)

Detail from a Nepalese *mani* stone, carved and painted with the Buddhist chant, *Om Mani Padme Hum* (Lotus *Mantra*). Chanting sacred texts or words is a method of approaching or attaining the humility necessary to reawaken our essential and primordial nature, since we are created in the image of God.

CATHOLIC ROSARIES

SINCE THE MIDDLE AGES, ROSARIES have represented an integral component of the act of praying within the Roman Catholic Church, after becoming a widely accepted and useful means of counting and remembering complex cycles of devotional prayers written in liturgical languages. In the 12th century, Christianity became the last major religion to adopt the use of prayer beads, a decision possibly influenced by frequent contact with the Arabs during the Holy Crusades or in Moorish Spain. It is also arguable that the use of such prayer-counters developed independently in the West, perhaps in Ireland, in response to the growing desire of congregations to keep track of an ever-expanding repertoire of prayers.

THE ROMAN CATHOLIC PRAYER TRADITION

The term "rosary" refers to the repetition of prayers as well as the string of beads on which prayers are actually recited. One of the many meanings of the word "rosary" is "wreath of roses", symbolising the string of prayers. The word derives from the Latin *rosarium*, or "rose garden", a contemplative place for meditation associated with the garden of Eden and Paradise.

The Roman Catholic rosary is recited for the greater glory of God, to honour the Blessed Virgin and for the good of all souls, including one's own.

The devotee recites the Lord's Prayer, or Our Father, followed by 10 Hail Marys upon the prayer beads, which number 150, as do the Psalms. In doing so, the believer participates in the Angelic Salutation spoken by the Angel Gabriel to the Virgin Mary at the Annunciation. The Apostle's Creed and the Doxology, or Glory Be, can also be stated with other beads and medals.

On specific days of the week and during certain liturgical seasons, the worshipper can choose to selectively meditate on the Joyful, Sorrowful and Glorious Mysteries, crucial events in the life of Christ and the Virgin, while reciting the rosary.

OPPORTUNITIES FOR PRAYER
Rosaries offer a portable access to prayer, a means of praising God wherever you happen to find yourself without necessarily having to attend Mass service. The believer can thus take time from the hectic pace of modern life to actively meditate on the example of the lives of Jesus and the Virgin and achieve a holier inner state through the solitude found in prayer.

"Do thou all within. And if perchance thou seekest some high place, some holy place, make thee a temple for God within."

ST AUGUSTINE
(354–430 CE)

DIFFERENT TYPES OF CATHOLIC ROSARIES

The full Roman Catholic rosary took its current form during the 16th century, when it was commonly known as a *paternoster*. Other Latin terms for prayer beads, such as *numeralia*, *computum* and *calculi*, bear witness to the intricacies of the act of counting. Numbering 150, the standard Catholic rosary features beads organised into 15 decades, or rows of 10 beads, which help the user to mark divisions between different prayers. A five-decade rosary (50 beads) is commonly used in these practices. A chaplet refers to any other number of beads on

A regular Catholic rosary comprises 150 *Ave*, or Hail Mary beads, 15 *Pater*, or Our Father beads, plus five lead-in beads representing the introductory prayers, such as the Glory Be.

a string and some prayer ropes may even have as few as 10 beads but, by passing the cord around each finger, devotees can easily count up to 50.

TYPES OF BEADS

As the essence and spiritual efficacy of rosary devotion within the Roman Catholic religion lies in the holy names that the prayers variously honour, it is apt that the most numerous beads on the rosary are *Ave*, or Hail Mary beads, in honour of the Blessed Virgin, Mother of God. These standard beads are interrupted by accent beads, which indicate where other prayers begin – the Our Father prayer, for instance – as well as by medals and crucifixes. The bead that lies at the base of the string is known as the holy Introit bead and forms the entrance into the circle of prayer.

Over the centuries, different types of rosaries and chaplets have emerged from various orders within the Church to facilitate the act of praying different combinations of prayers. The Brigittine rosary, for example, features seven Our Father beads plus 63 Hail Mary beads to mark the Virgin's age. Compare this with the Franciscan Crown of Our Lady rosary, whose 72 Hail Mary beads are also said to signify the years of her life. The Crown of Our Lord rosary is made up of 33 Our Father beads to celebrate Christ's years on earth, plus five Hail Mary beads to represent His wounds. Some families still keep a tradition of long, oversized rosaries which allow each family member to join in the rosary prayers simultaneously. Praying together as a family is a practice that the Catholic Church is increasingly keen to promote and encourage in the 21st century as a means of strengthening the identity of the Roman Catholic family nucleus.

HOLY MATERIALS

Through the course of history, regional folklore and local beliefs have combined to attach particular mystical meanings and protective connotations to both the colour, appearance and substance of various gemstones and other materials used to make rosary beads. To boost the sacred essence of rosaries even further, Catholics often ask for them to be blessed by prayer or with holy water by priests.

THE CRUCIFIX

This visual reminder of Christ's Crucifixion can be made of simple wood or precious metals. Ivory crosses were favoured in earlier times, because the colour white was associated with the Virgin and moral fortitude. Silver in Christian thought has come to represent purity and chastity, and its propensity to tarnish when neglected reflects the need for the pious to cleanse the heart through regular devotion.

Olive pits, or olive-wood beads, have a long-standing historical significance for Christians, recalling the reconciliation of God with Man after the Biblical flood. In Greek, the same root gives the words "olive" and "mercy". Olive rosaries acquired in Jerusalem, for example, refer back to the event of Christ's withdrawal into the olive grove of Gethsemane on the Mount of Olives on the eve of his Crucifixion.

Roses, among all types of flowers, are considered to be the only blooms to successfully yield rosary beads from their petals due to a high oil content. Worthy of note, from the 15th century onwards, is the rose's rich symbolic associations with the Virgin Mary.

Coral beads have been highly valued for their protective powers since the Middle Ages. Rosary beads made from coral are also thought to encourage wisdom.

Pearls are considered to be natural symbols of perfection and purity, developing as they do from the imperfection of a grain of sand. Pearls signal wisdom, understood not as intelligence, but as *Hagia Sophia* – a sacred knowing.

Amethyst is regarded as the stone of piety and mental balance. Its distinctive colour is associated with a high state of spirituality.

Topaz, according to St Hildegard (1098–1179 CE), was a cure for eyesight problems, which could also be interpreted as a metaphor for achieving religious insight.

Sapphire, perhaps because its colour recalls the celestial realm most, made early Christian theologians believe that holding their gaze on this gemstone could elevate their thoughts from the earthly realm into a more heavenly dimension.

Bloodstone, with its red speckles, recalls the blood of Christ. Rosary beads made from this type of stone bring peace and understanding.

Renaissance master Piero della Francesca's famous 15th-century Montefeltro altarpiece painting bears witness to the ubiquity of the rosary motif in Roman Catholic visual iconography: the sleeping Christ child, surrounded by angels and saints, is portrayed wearing a rosary made of coral, prized for its protective powers in many world cultures.

*"Would you like me to tell you a 'secret'?
It is simple, and after all, is no secret.
Pray, pray much. Say the rosary every day."*
POPE JOHN PAUL II
(1920– CE)

Praying with the rosary...

Starting to Pray

Begin in a prayerful position, holding the crucifix in your right hand. Focus on the meaning of the words rather than allowing the prayers to become a mechanical repetition which is simply learned by rote rather than truly felt.

1 Make the sign of the cross with the crucifix, saying, "In the Name of the Father, and of the Son, and of the Holy Spirit. Amen." Kiss the crucifix. Recite the Apostle's Creed (*see page 31*).

2 Take the first bead following the crucifix and pray one Our Father. On each of the next three beads, pray the Hail Mary (*see opposite*).

3 On the next bead, pray the Doxology (*see opposite*). This marks the end of the introductory prayers.

4 Still holding that bead, pray one Our Father. On each of the next 10 beads, pray one Hail Mary, while meditating on the Mysteries (*see pages 28–29*). After completing 10 Hail Marys, pray the Doxology (*see opposite*) on the next large bead and, if desired, the Fatima Prayer (*see page 31*).

5 Each succeeding decade is performed in the same way: one Our Father, 10 Hail Marys as you meditate, then the Doxology (*see opposite*) and, if desired, the Fatima Prayer (*see page 31*).

CATHOLIC ROSARIES

26

Our Father

"Our Father, who art in heaven, hallowed be Thy Name. Thy kingdom come. Thy will be done on earth as it is in heaven. Give us this day our daily bread and forgive us our trespasses as we forgive those who trespass against us. And lead us not into temptation, but deliver us from evil. Amen."

Hail Mary

"Hail Mary, full of grace, the Lord is with thee. Blessed art thou amongst women and blessed is the fruit of thy womb, Jesus. Holy Mary, Mother of God, pray for us sinners, now, and at the hour of our death. Amen."

Doxology (Glory Be)

"Glory be to the Father, and to the Son, and to the Holy Spirit. As it was in the beginning, is now and ever shall be, world without end. Amen."

Praying with the rosary...

The Mysteries

The five decades of beads on the rosary correspond to three sets of five Mysteries based on events in the life of Christ and the Virgin Mary. On specific days (*see below*), these Joyful, Sorrowful and Glorious Mysteries are meditated on with each decade of the rosary.

Mysteries of the Rosary

The Joyful Mysteries (The Creation)
Mondays and Thursdays; Sundays from the first Sunday of Advent until Lent

The Annunciation
The Visitation
The Nativity of Christ
The Presentation in the Temple
The Finding in the Temple

The Sorrowful Mysteries (The Fall)
Tuesdays and Fridays; Sundays in Lent

The Agony in the Garden
The Scourging at the Pillar
The Crowning with Thorns
The Carrying of the Cross
The Crucifixion

The Glorious Mysteries (The Redemption)
Wednesdays and Saturdays; Sundays from Easter until Advent

The Resurrection
The Ascension
The Descent of the Holy Spirit
The Assumption
The Coronation of Mary

1 After completing the introductory prayers *(see steps 1–3, pages 26–27)*, take the first bead of the first decade and meditate on the first Mystery for that day. For example, for the Joyful Mysteries, begin with the Annunciation, thinking, "I desire the love of humility" while imagining the state of Mary when the Angel Gabriel greeted her. In this way, you practise the virtue of humility based on the perfect example of Mary. Say one Our Father, one Hail Mary for each subsequent bead, and after the tenth bead, say the Doxology and, if desired, the Fatima Prayer *(see page 31)*.

2 In the same way, meditate on a further Joyful Mystery with each decade. Thinking of each one while repeating the Hail Marys encourages you to establish charity through the Visitation, the love of God through the Nativity of Christ, sacrifice through the Presentation and fervour with the Finding in The Temple. At the end of the decade, say the Doxology and the Fatima Prayer *(see page 31)*.

3 When contemplating the Sorrowful Mysteries, repentance is encouraged by meditating on the Agony in the Garden, mortification by the Scourging at the Pillar, moral courage by the Crowning with Thorns, patience and humility at the Carrying of the Cross and final perseverance at the Crucifixion.

4 By meditating on the Glorious Mysteries, faith is strengthened through the Resurrection, hope is instilled with the Ascension and the other mysteries encourage fervency, a joyful death and love of Mary.

5 After finishing the five decades, say a concluding prayer on the medal, usually Hail, Holy Queen *(see page 30)*. Make the sign of the cross and kiss the crucifix.

Praying with the rosary...

Key Prayers

Hail, Holy Queen

"*Hail, Holy Queen, Mother of mercy, our life, our sweetness and our hope. To thee do we cry, poor banished children of Eve. To thee do we send up our sighs, mourning and weeping in this valley of tears. Turn then, most gracious advocate, thine eyes of mercy towards us. And after this our exile, show unto us the blessed fruit of thy womb, Jesus. O clement, O loving, O sweet Virgin Mary. Pray for us, O holy Mother of God. That we may be made worthy of the promises of Christ. Let us pray: O God, whose only-begotten Son, by His life, death and resurrection, has purchased for us the rewards of eternal life, grant, we beseech You, that meditating upon these Mysteries of the Holy Rosary of the Blessed Virgin Mary, we may imitate what they contain, and obtain what they promise, through the same Christ, our Lord. Amen.*"

ORTHODOX ROSARIES

ON THE SIMPLE WOOLLEN ROPE OF knots that forms the Orthodox rosary, the Jesus Prayer is recited. This practice is used as an aid to inner attentiveness, breath control and prostrations, all of which are integral parts of this rite. Greek Orthodox monks living in monasteries perched on holy Mount Athos on the peninsula of Athos dedicate their lives to the pursuit of *hesychia*, a silence or a stilling of the heart. This spiritual quest leads to union with God. Such traditions of mysticism were lost for centuries in the Christianity of the West. But new conservative movements in the Anglican and Episcopalian Churches, and those keen to explore the spiritual practices of the early Celtic saints, are rediscovering ways of making this type of contemplative inner journey possible through the use of prayer beads.

PRAYER RITES IN THE ORTHODOX CHURCH

For centuries, the Eastern Orthodox Church has used the Jesus Prayer in conjunction with the knotted woollen rosary. St Isaac the Syrian (338–439 CE) described it as a prayer which transcends a series of physical acts to become a state of *being*. You endeavour to accomplish St Paul's commandment of "pray[ing] without ceasing" (1 Thessalonians 5:17). *Kyrie Iesu Christi* (Lord Jesus Christ), *Huie Theou* (Son of God), *eleison emas* (have mercy on us) or *eleison me* (have mercy on me) are repeated on each knot of the rosary.

ATTAINING GODLINESS

The purpose of life on earth for Orthodox Christians is to prepare for union with the Divine. This is achieved by regularly receiving the Sacraments, following God's Commandments and living virtuously through prayer. Because we are made in the image and likeness of God, by withdrawing within and examining the heart, all of us can perfect our Divine potentiality and dwell in God as He dwells in us.

The Jesus Prayer is a particularly powerful way to find God because Christ rests at its centre, effectively Christ unified with God: his mortality represents the path of every man towards a reunion with God. As the name Jesus is believed to have the presence and energy of God inherent within it, so in repeating His name, you partake in the nature of the Divine through utterance.

USING THE BREATH

Someone chanting or saying *Kyrie eleison* (Lord have mercy, Christ have mercy) remains in a passive state, as when receiving the Holy Communion. But repeating the words as part of the Jesus Prayer forces the worshipper into a more active engagement, whereby the aspirant struggles for instruction and spiritual direction as he or she concentrates on the repetition of the uttered words.

Breath control and postures are given as part of spiritual direction. The regulated breath supports the invocation, yoking mind, body and emotions to the act of

The interior of this tiny church on the island of Naxos, Greece, vividly conveys the devotional privacy which still characterises prayer and worship rites within the Greek Orthodox faith.

praying. Concentration on the breath recalls God breathing life into Adam in the Book of Genesis. Each inhalation rekindles the Holy Spirit within. *Ruach*, the Hebrew word for "spirit", also signifies "breath" or "air". The Arabic word *nff* also stands for both "soul" and "breath", while *ruh* means "spirit".

The Hesychast method sometimes introduces prostration to the practice as a way of intensifying the elevated state achieved through prayer. Spiritual guidance comes from study of the Scriptures, the reading of spiritual authors such as the Desert Fathers found in the *Philokalia* (1782) and from masters or elders: in Greek, *geron*; in Russian, *staretz*; in Arabic, *sheikh*. Currently there is difficulty in finding spiritual directors due to a widespread shortage of priests.

THE PRAYER OF THE HEART

In 1782, the *Philokalia,* a collection of writings in Greek setting out the thoughts of Orthodox Christian spiritual masters

Greek Orthodox monks are presented with their own individual prayer ropes as part of their investiture ceremony into the monastic order. These ecclesiastics will come to pray the prayer rope between 80 and 100 times a day.

from the 4th to the 15th century, was published. In it are related the experiences of saints such as Gregory of Sinai (590–604 CE) with the Jesus Prayer and descriptions of the life of the Hesychast. When this work was eventually translated into Russian, its increased circulation helped establish the Prayer of the Heart within the Russian Orthodox Church as well.

This alternative name for the Jesus Prayer describes the interior journey taken by the devotee using the prayer rope. Saying the words on each inhalation and exhalation while using the knots on the rope helps the devout to withdraw from the outside world and focus on the spirit within, preparing the heart to experience an emptiness filled only with God's presence. Through repetition, the words resonate in the heart as a living prayer, ensuring that Christ resides within.

The classic religious work, *The Way of A Pilgrim* (1930), is a wonderful introduction to the Jesus Prayer. In his search for a life of "unceasing prayer", an anonymous 19th-century pilgrim is taken on by a spiritual master, who assigns him a transforming number of Jesus Prayers to be said daily. As a result, the reader encounters a perfect example of faith and humility engendered by true spirituality.

THE SILENT ORTHODOX PRAYER ROPE

The knotted woollen prayer rope, known as *metanoia,* literally "change of mind" or *kombologion* ("string of knots") in the Greek tradition, contains 33, 50 or, most commonly, 100 knots. In the Russian Orthodox equivalent, the *chotki*, 33,100 or even 300 knots are common. In contrast to the Roman Catholic rosary, the knots are not divided into decades, or other such groupings, and are used silently. Orthodox bead rosaries may also be employed in prayer and feature an equal number of beads and knots. These are often strung by monks from readily available natural materials, such as olive pits, nuts or shells, or they may be fashioned from wood.

Tradition has it that rosaries developed from finger-counting or from moving pebbles from one pile to another as a way of remembering, marking repetitions or focusing the mind. It proved simple to tie knots along the length of a piece of rope to create a portable counting device which made prayer accessible anywhere.

Orthodox Crosses

The Orthodox rosary cross differs in shape from the Catholic crucifix. Its lower strut represents the fact that one good thief went to heaven, while the other was relegated to hell after refusing to repent on the day of Christ's Crucifixion. The Constantine cross incorporates the Greek letters *chi* and *rho*, the first two letters for Christ in the Greek alphabet. The Russian Orthodox cross can also take another form, which includes stylised bars to represent the inscription and footrest beneath the crucifix.

Praying with the prayer rope...

The Jesus Prayer

"If the soul is vigilant and withdraws from all distractions, and abandons its own will, then the spirit of God invades it."

ABBA CRONIUS (285–386 CE)

By regulating the pattern of inhalations and exhalations with the rhythm of the repeated words, this prayer coordinated with the breath provides a way of entering within to empty yourself and experience unity with God. At its simplest, the Jesus Prayer can be used to calm both mind and body during times of stress. At its most profound, it serves those seeking ultimate reality. This type of prayer may include external postures, such as bowing or prostration, under the careful and necessary guidance of a spiritual master. It is important that the words be recited slowly, with serious intent and absolute devotion. This helps you to focus on the realm of the spirit and empty yourself for the Divine presence: in order for the ocean to enter, you must descend below sea-level first.

The Jesus Prayer

"Lord Jesus Christ, Son of God, have mercy on me."

1 On the in-breath, at the first knot of the rosary, say "Lord Jesus Christ, Son of God". Speak slowly, letting the words fill one complete inhalation. Begin by reciting the words out loud but gradually learn to internalise them until they can be recited in silence.

2 On the out-breath, say "Have mercy on me". Moving on to the next bead, repeat the phrase on both the in- and out-breaths, working through each knot on the rosary in the same way. It is essential to be conscious of every uttered word and return to the contents of the prayer each time your thoughts stray. Both the mind and heart must be attentive, joined in effortless prayer.

3 Under the supervision of a spiritual guide, you may be instructed to add prostrations to your normal breathing pattern, either by bowing from the waist or lying face down on the floor. Praying with the body in this way helps the mind and heart to focus more intently on the prayer itself. It is important that the physical movements should not distract from the words which are being uttered.

THE ANGLICAN PRAYER BEAD ROPE

Invoking the name of Jesus using the prayer rope has commonly been thought of as exclusive to the Eastern Orthodox Church yet it has always been part of Christian life in the West, too. An increasing number of worshippers in the Anglican and Episcopalian Churches on both sides of the Atlantic today continue the tradition of this overlooked practice. Since the 1980s, beads and invocatory prayer have been increasingly included as a support for meditation by contemplative prayer groups, such as the Centering Prayer Movement in the United States.

The Anglican prayer bead rope combines features from the Catholic rosary as well as from the Orthodox prayer rope by its containing 33 beads to represent Christ's years on earth. The founders of the Anglican Prayer Movement make reference to the traditions of the early Desert *Ammas* (Mothers) and *Abbas* (Fathers) who wove baskets or plaited rope as a method for focusing their minds on prayer while they made a living. Many of the rosaries available

today are crafted and strung by those who follow a life of relative seclusion dedicated to contemplation and prayer.

FINDING THE STILL POINT
Cistercian monk Abbot Thomas Keating (1923– CE), a leading figure of the Centering Prayer Movement in the United States, has traced the history of the deeper meditative traditions of Christian prayer by his study of lost mystical methods, such as those used by Julian of Norwich (1342–1416 CE) and medieval Christian monks, who spoke of their contemplative prayer techniques as "entering the cloud of unknowing". This rediscovered tradition has inspired Keating to introduce new prayer techniques, the aim being that of teaching ways of unblocking unconscious emotional patterns which prevent the deepening of spiritual development.

Such prayer techniques help draw the devotee into a deeply contemplative state in which negative thought patterns and emotions come to be discarded and inner freedom is won as one learns to "rest in

God". As the tradition is so recent, there are no official prayers which can be said just by using Anglican prayer beads, although the Jesus Prayer *(see pages 40–41)* is often uttered, as are extracts from *The Book of Common Prayer* (1662).

TYPES OF BEADS

The grouping of prayer beads in the Anglican rosary is rich in symbolism. These prayer beads tend to have four groupings, each composed of seven beads, known as weeks, which are divided by four cruciform beads. The weeks signify the number of days taken to create the universe; the temporal week; the seasons comprising the Church year and the Sacraments. The four cruciform beads represent Christ's Crucifixion but also stand for the seasons and the compass directions North, South, East and West. An Invitatory bead guides the worshipper into the prayer cycle in the same way that the Invitatory or Opening Psalm ushers the faithful into their daily office.

The Anglican rosary is a relatively new type of prayer which combines elements from the Roman Catholic rosary and the Orthodox Jesus Prayer. The 33-bead design came into existence through a process of prayerful spiritual exploration in the context of a contemplative prayer group.

CELTIC CHRISTIAN PRAYER

Modern Western Christians in Northern Europe and North America are rediscovering the contemplative meditation practices of the early Celtic saints who established Christian ways of worship, distinct from those of the Roman Catholic Church, in Ireland, Cornwall, Wales, Brittany and Scotland. The roots of Celtic Christianity are to be found in the community that grew around the Apostle John (died *c.* 100 CE) in Ephesus, modern-day Turkey, as well as the lives of the desert monastics, the *Ammas* and *Abbas*. People exploring Celtic traditions today might use a 150-bead rosary based on the original Catholic template, and also use the prayers associated with it.

Prayer in the Celtic Christian tradition celebrates the sanctity of all ecological life, nature and the seasons. For Celtic Christians, the natural world represents one continuous prayer: each river, tree and mountain contains a Divine spark. Every person and every thing is part of,

The distinctive circle behind the points of a Celtic cross is an ancient symbol denoting the interconnectedness of everything in the universe, the sun and eternity. The cross itself represents the four corners of the earth.

and plays a part in, the great circle of life. Prayer helps adherents enter this circle and become aware of the invisible "other world" whence all things originate and will, eventually, return.

Prayer beads support the Celtic Christian journey into this inner world of devotion. The repetitive geometric pattern of the beads leads the eye and mind away from the material world into a place of contemplation. The knots between beads evoke the great Celtic tradition of knotwork and symbolise a line without beginning or end. This is identical to the eternal circle created by the rosary and the circular, repetitive form of the prayers it requires. Other special beads might include the shamrock shape, in remembrance of St Patrick (390–461 CE), who likened it to the Holy Trinity.

Although all branches of Christianity honour the Virgin Mary and Jesus, reflecting both the feminine and masculine aspects of God, the feminine essence of the Divine is greatly respected in all Celtic Christian writings, and may be evident in Celtic rosaries in the form of the four-legged St Brigid's (451–525 CE) cross, usually made in silver to resemble the original, rush-woven one. Celtic Christianity generally has more in common with the Eastern Orthodox faith than with the Western Roman tradition.

THE
JEWISH
TEFILLIN

THE PRAYER STRAPS OF THE TEFILLIN
literally bind the Commandments of God (written on
parchment scrolls contained in cuboid leather *batim* boxes)
to the arm and the head. This act demonstrates humility in
serving God by disciplining and sublimating the desires of
the heart, body and mind. When a Jew repeats sacred
passages while wearing these boxes and straps, he or she is
metaphorically following what is known as a *sutra* in
Sanskrit, at once a "thread" (like the straps) and a
"commandment of wisdom" (like those written on
parchment inside the boxes). In the words of King
Solomon, "Bind them upon thy fingers, write them upon
the table of thine heart" (Proverbs 7:3).

UNDERSTANDING THE JEWISH TEFILLIN

"Tefillin are very holy. While man wears them on his head and arm, he is humble, G-d-fearing, he will not be frivolous, speak idle talk, or think impure thoughts. Rather he thinks about truth and righteousness."

RAMBAM, MITZVOS, LILCHOS TEFILLIN (4:25)

The bejewelled cover of this *Sefer Torah* is inscribed with the tablets bearing God's 10 Commandments.

Judaic practice focuses not on counting rosary beads like other religions, but on wearing the *tefillin*, composed of two sets of leather *batim* boxes (containing passages from the Torah) tied to the head and the arm by means of leather *retzuos* straps. Pious Jews bind these *tefillin* boxes, considered to be like prayers, to the body: one is worn on the forehead (the head *tefillin*) and the other around the left arm (the arm *tefillin*), very close to the heart. Finally, the strap is coiled around the fingers and palm in such a way as to make it form the letter *yod*, which stands for the Ineffable

Name, and the letter *esh*, which represents *Shaddai*, the Eternal One.

THE TWO *BATIM* BOXES

The first leather box, the *bayis shel yad,* is strapped around the arm and contains four verses from the Torah – two from Exodus, two from Deuteronomy – written on a single piece of parchment. Because it is traditionally believed that it is harder to discipline the body than the mind, it is bound on first and needs to stay in place for longer. This arm *tefillin* sits as close as possible to the heart and prompts the wearer to remember to keep physical temptation in check, the hands representing the ability to take action as well as being associated with the sense of touch, or sensuality.

The second case, the *bayis shel rosh*, is bound to the head and contains four inscriptions from the Torah written out on individual pieces of parchment kept in separate compartments. It assists the wearer in harnessing the intellect as well as the senses. Because it is secured with a knot that sits at the top of the spine, this part of the *tefillin* provides a prompt with each movement to bring every part of the body into consciousness of God.

Binding on the two types of *batim* boxes serves as a symbolic ceremonial route by which to overwhelm the pull of the body and intellect, the senses and the desire for action. In centring the worshipper inside the heart and head, wearing the *tefillin* helps to focus within, enabling a humble and uninterrupted contemplation of God's Commandments.

THE *RETZUOS* STRAPS

Retzuos are cords made of leather, 10–11mm in width, cut at an angle at the ends and coloured black with paint or ink. Black is a significant

colour because it is does not alter, just as the pious remain constant and steadfast in their devotions. The straps stretch and crack with use and, as it is vital that no raw leather is exposed by cracks, they are usually replaced every five to 10 years. When wrapped, *retzuos* straps must stay in immediate contact with the skin. Clothing, even spectacles, would interrupt this direct line to God. When hanging, the longer right-hand strap reaches to the point of circumcision while the left-hand strap touches the navel, both reminders of the need to sublimate physical pleasures to the will of God.

Leather *tefillin* boxes contain passages from the Torah. Secured to the head and arm by means of *retzuos* straps, they are worn by Jewish males on weekdays for the duration of the morning service. This ancient religious practice serves as a living symbol of God's relationship with the Israelites.

OBEYING GOD'S COMMANDMENTS

"Let everyone cry out to God and lift his heart up to God, as if he were hanging by a hair in a tempest."

HASIDIC TALE

The word *tefillin* is related to the Hebrew *tefilah*, or "prayer", and derives from the root *pe-lamed-lamed* and the word *l'hitpalel*, meaning "to judge oneself". By entering within through prayer, the devout Jew judges him- or herself against Holy Law.

THE WORD OF GOD

The verses placed in the protective leather cases of the *tefillin* are taken from verses in the Torah – the first five books of the Bible – that refer to God's Commandment to hear His Divine words. They serve as a reminder that God freed the Jews from bondage and commanded, "And thou shalt love the Lord thy God with all thine heart, and with all thy soul, and with all thy might." (Deuteronomy 6:5) and "Therefore shall ye lay up these My words in your heart and in your soul, and bind them for a sign upon your hand, that they may be as frontlets between your eyes" (Deuteronomy 11:18). It is said that because all the materials forming the *tefillin* are technically edible – leather, parchment wrapped in calf's tail hair – these words of God could literally be "absorbed" by the devout.

Wearing the *tefillin* thus places the devotee in a state of constant awareness of God's presence. Known as "the Glory of Israel", the leather cases and straps serve as both a visual and tactile sign that one is heeding God's Commandments, seeking to conquer the temptation of worldly pleasure and, through contemplative prayer, deepen spiritual practice.

The tradition of wearing the *tefillin* has helped the Jewish community maintain links with age-old practices which have survived across the centuries and continents.

"And thou shalt bind them for a sign upon thine hand, and they shall be as frontlets between thine eyes."

DEUTERONOMY 6:8

VENERATING THE DIVINE

The aim of spiritual practice in Judaism is *kedushah*, or holiness, and it is a way of life. It is commonly believed that every life experience offers an opportunity to increase awareness of God and engender spirituality through prayer. The possibilities are endless: everyday activities such as eating, working, getting dressed, going to bed and getting up can all take on a spiritual dimension.

By uttering traditional blessings at these times, known as *berakot*, any Jew can ignite in everyday, habitual actions and events the spark of the Divine that lies within them – for instance, on hearing thunder, one might proclaim, "Blessed are you, O Lord, our God! King of the Universe, whose power and might fill the universe".

Jewish mystical thought holds that God's presence lies hidden inside every part of the physical universe. Indeed, the Hebrew word for "universe" derives from an etymological root meaning "to conceal". The numerous blessings release the Divine within, bridging heaven and earth and helping to reveal God's presence in the world. Such quotidian acts present opportunities to approach and glorify the Divine. Residing within, transcending the moment and individual desires, and looking at oneself objectively with a view to rectifying mistakes are part of this way of experiencing the connectedness and sanctity of all forms of life. Such constant prayerful attention, or *kavanah*, is a prerequisite for meaningful prayer.

This Jewish boy has recently celebrated his *barmitzvah* and come of age. He is now eligible to wear the *tefillin* leather boxes and straps. During the sacred ritual of donning the hand and head *tefillin*, he cannot speak or even gesticulate.

INSIDE THE TEFILLIN

"Hear O Israel, the Lord our God is one Lord: Blessed be His glorious kingdom for ever and ever."
OPENING LINES OF THE *SHEMA*, FUNDAMENTAL PROCLAMATION OF THE JEWISH FAITH

Tefillin are regarded as one of the principal symbols of Judaism and are one of just three objects considered to be holy by their very nature. The other two sacred objects are the Torah scrolls and the *mezzuzah* parchments attached to the thresholds of dwellings. Like all the holy symbols and ritual objects of Judaism, *tefillin* encompass, in their very being, the history and symbolism of the Jews for the Jewish Diaspora – the Judaic community around the world. Simply to look upon such sacred objects is a reminder of the spiritual path and entices the mind and emotions to engage on a sacred journey towards a more profound awareness of the world. In many of the world's great religions, the mind uses such physical objects as intermediaries in its quest for ineffable truths and the intangible.

FOLK MYTHOLOGY

Tefillin are reputed in Jewish folklore to offer Divine protection to both body and soul. Jewish men with financial or relationship problems, or difficulties in the workplace, are readily advised to have the state of their *tefillin* verified by a *tefillin*-checker. Numerous word-of-mouth stories tell of miraculous resolutions to problems occurring once cracked prayer straps or damaged paintwork on the *tefillin* have been restored.

SACRED NUMBERS

Numerology in Judaism is greatly significant. Within the *tefillin*, the five hollow *chalalim*, or compartments for parchment inscriptions – four in the leather head box, one in the arm box – represent the number of senses which must be subdued to become closer to God. The 12 stitches threaded through each box recall the number of angels surrounding the throne of heaven and the tribes of Israel which gathered around the temple of Jerusalem. Calculations based on the number of parts belonging to the two types of cases total 613 – the number of *mitzvos*, or

Commandments, in the Torah. *Tefillin* represent in very physical form what God wills for the human soul.

VERIFYING THE SCRIPTURES
Every part of the *tefillin* is subjected to exacting checks to verify that each is indeed "kosher". Particular attention is paid to the state of the parchment inscriptions – two verses from Exodus, two from Deuteronomy – handwritten by a master *sofer* (scribe) on *parshios* (parchment),

usually made of lambskin rolled up and inserted into the *batim* leather boxes in a prescribed order. Although different Jewish traditions, such as the Sephardic (Spanish and Portuguese) and Ashkenazic (Central and Eastern European), use varying forms of script, the laws governing all lettering are stringent. If any of the obligatory 1,594 characters are missing, incorrectly written or touching, the *tefillin* is declared *posul*, or invalid, by the *tefillin*-checker.

Venerated in the Jewish community, the *tefillin*-checker is allowed to open up the *batim* boxes of the *tefillin* to inspect the state of the parchment script inside. He also examines the condition of the leather *retzuos* straps and the shape of the *batim* boxes.

Praying with the tefillin...

Binding the Words of God

Tefillin **are worn during weekday morning services by Jewish males over the age of 13, usage being obligatory after the celebration of the *barmitzvah* (coming-of-age ceremony). In recent years, non-Orthodox women have also adopted their use. While binding the leather boxes around the head and arm with the prayer straps, the person praying may repeat the words set out opposite.**

1 The arm *tefillin* is tightened around the bicep of one's left arm, wrapped seven or eight times around one's lower arm, then passed three times around one's middle finger. The end is secured by being tucked underneath.

2 The head *tefillin* is then placed approximately one finger's width above one's hairline, so that it sits in line with the centre of one's eyes.

3 The *kesher*, or knot, passes over one's head to rest on the back of it, at the base of one's skull and the nape of one's neck. Before adjusting the knot, one states the intention to move the knot to make the *tefillin* more holy: *l'shem keduchas tefillin*.

4 The straps hang down as follows: the right strap ending at the site of circumcision, the left at one's navel.

5 Wearing the *tefillin* allows for meditation on the *mitzvos*, or Commandments, and helps the aspirant to enter within and surrender the mind, body, senses and heart for the sake of God.

" *I am here, intent upon the act of putting on the tefillin...that declares the absolute unity of God and reminds us of the miracles and wonders which He wrought for us when He brought us out of Egypt...He has commanded us to lay the tefillin upon the hand as a memorial of His outstretched arm, opposite the heart, to indicate the duty of subjecting the longing and desires of our heart to His service. Blessed be He.* "

HINDU MALAS

IN HINDUISM, THE WORLD'S OLDEST faith, prayer beads, or *malas*, are used for the repetition of a *mantra* or Divine names through the devotional act known as *japa yoga*. Sculptures illustrating this type of practice have been found dating back to the Mauryan Shunga dynasty (185–73 BCE) in northern India. These works of art are a testament to humanity's long-standing preoccupation with overcoming temporal attachments: through the repetition of sacred names on *malas,* sin is cancelled out and worldly distractions are minimised. By constantly invoking holy names and syllables thus, the devotee is brought closer to the presence of God, and in so doing, discovers the true nature of humankind, which is pure, eternal and free.

LIBERATING THE SOUL

Life's aim for a Hindu is liberation and self-realisation, or *moksha*, final union with the Supreme; it is reached by service, devotion and total self-surrender. On the Hindu *mala*, devotees recite sacred formulae-*mantras* or the names of deities.

Mantra recitations are considered to erase sin from within and sanctify the worshipper. Chanting the holy names of Divine incarnations, such as *Rama* or *Krishna*, is believed to transform the physical body into a spiritual body, thereby enabling the believer to reach *ananda*, a state of transcendental bliss, in which the ego merges with God.

AIMS OF PRAYER

Through *sadhana* – devotional meditation or prayer – the exterior world of duplicity and separateness is left behind. While mind and body are respectively occupied with the movement of beads and the repetition of a single word or phrase, one withdraws into a place of stillness and completeness. Dualities, such as inside and outside, male and female, presence and absence, body and soul, begin to dissolve. An attempt is made to achieve the realisation – *samadhi* – of the interconnectedness of all things, which are part of the same Divine Essence. Such knowledge helps the faithful comprehend how *Brahman*, all-pervading God, is actually also manifest in *Atman*, the self, and in every other thing, as expounded in the *Upanishads* (800–400 BCE), religious treatises composed by Indian Vedic sages.

ROLE OF THE *MALA*

Using *malas* creates a devotional focus and a concentration of attention – of the body with finger movements, of the mind with invocations. The object and its accompanying rituals, such as washing before use and the lighting of candles and incense, prepare the soul to leave the everyday and enter a sacred dimension. In counting beads, you measure out the immeasurable, where dualities and a sense of the horizontal dimension cease.

This young naked *sadhu* at the Khumba Mela (Great Urn Festival), held every 12 years in Allahabad in India, belongs to a special sect of Shiva devotees. His body and face are smeared in ash; his uncut hair is swept up in a turban bearing sacred words. Around his neck is a crystal *mala* and *rudraksha* beads.

THE SACRED ASSOCIATIONS OF THE HINDU MALA

The Hindu *mala* is composed of 108 separate beads, with an extra *meru* bead and a tassel marking the beginning of the cycle. The word *meru* recalls the mythological holy mountain at the centre of the Hindu cosmic universe and Lord Vishnu's heavenly seat. A sacred number in Hinduism, 108 marks the 12 astrological houses and nine planets of the Solar System.

Like Christian and Muslim terms for prayer beads, *mala* signifies a rose, a garden or a heavenly garland. Such meanings attest to its ability to transport the believer into the heart's garden and offer blossoms to its deities. The *mala*'s circular form operates as a microcosmic reminder of the universe's endless and fluid continuity. In marking off beads with the fingers, one gets a sense of *lila*, the rhythmic play of the universe, and in so doing, start to merge with the Divine presence. The Hindu universe is thought of as orderly and cyclical: using the *mala* allows the worshipper to experience this cosmic order in its immense complexity.

SACRED MATERIALS
No material is regarded as too lowly or precious to form *mala* beads; a stone daubed with paint on an Indian wayside shrine is revered as highly as the most finely carved and richly adorned temple

Primarily used for counting prayers, the 108-beaded Hindu *mala* is perceived as inseparable from any deity it is used to invoke. Not a piece of jewellery, like a talisman it is said to absorb the power and motivations of its rightful owner. Treated with care and respect, its magnetism will increase proportionally.

"The Name pronounced even once is a benefit, whether one is aware of it or not. Prayer is not verbal, it is from the heart. To merge into the heart is prayer."

SRI RAMANA MAHARSHI (1879–1950 CE)

deity. Certain materials, however, have inevitably become associated with the worship of specific deities.

Wood is the first choice for *malas*, as it is for temple buildings, with sandalwood from Mysore ever popular. Vishnu worshippers use *malas* of small beads carved from the stem of the *tulsi* (holy basil) shrub. Thought to be the source of life's elixir, *tulsi* ("incomparable one") is honoured in household shrines. Its sacred associations predate Hinduism, but the history of the plant is so entwined with the mythology of Vishnu that each year, it is ceremonially married to the deity. A *Krishna* bead caps the 108-bead strand, exalting Vishnu's eighth reincarnation. The dairymaids, or *gopis*, who surrendered devotion to Krishna, also amount to 108.

Rudraksha, the dried berries of the *Elaeocarpus ganitrus roxburgii* tree, have been associated with Hindu worship for at least 7,000 years, especially with Lord Shiva, and *rudraksha mala* beads are still used by devotees today. Each costly bead has several natural facets, or "mouths", most often five, all representing separate Divine qualities. Held to be the tears of Shiva, *rudraksha* beads have a rough texture analogous to the ascetic's austere lifestyle of *sannyasi*, whereby all wordly possessions are renounced for an itinerant existence.

Semi-precious stones, too, are considered suitable for *malas*, linking as they do deities with planets in *jyotish*, the Indian system of astrology. Ruby, for example, is the stone of the Sun and of Brahma.

THE POWER OF DEVOTION

A holy text, the *Rosary Upanishad* (800–400 BCE), prescribes a consecratory rite to spiritually endow the *mala*, which is thought to grow in spiritual potency with use by drawing energy from the reverence it is accorded. All *malas*, especially old ones or those used by holy men, are treated with special respect. If they touch the floor or another person, they are ritually cleansed. Care should be taken to never let *malas* be handled as objects of idle curiosity.

MANTRA YOGA

"Om *tunes the entire human being with the eternal music of the Divine, bringing the soul in direct contact with the in-dwelling and all-pervading Reality."*

SWAMI RAMDAS
(1884–1963 CE)

The Sanskrit word *mantra* derives from *manas* (mind) and *trai*, "to free from", "deliver" or "protect". A *mantra* literally protects the mind and frees it from the world. It is not an end in itself, but a way to approach the ultimate truth. "*Mantra* is a combination of words that stand for the Supreme Reality", states Swami Ramdas (1884–1963 CE), who had such absolute faith that when a monkey ran off with his glasses, he exclaimed, "God must be about to restore my sight!"

In Indian Vedic tradition, *mantras* have such a unique blend of sounds that the vibrational energy released through their repetition, or *japa*, out loud or soundlessly, sets up a pattern of reactions in the mind and body that may assist spiritual transformation, bringing man more in tune with God.

There are three types of *mantras*: abstract sounds such as *Om,* which refer to or identify with the Absolute, invocations of specific deities and seed *mantras* derived from Sanskrit sounds.

A *mantra* should originally be chosen and bestowed by a guru or *mantrakara* (mantra-maker), handed down from the guru to his disciple through the generations intact from the original ancient *rishi* (seer) who first received it. The strict rules which govern the sound's pronunciation and duration, pitch and intonation ensure that a *mantra* is preserved in its vibrant, original form.

CHANTING *OM*
Considered the primordial sound from which the universe itself flows, *Om* (pronounced "Aah-ooo-mmm") is considered to be the original source of all language, the one eternal syllable in which past, present and future simultaneously exist. No *mantra* is more powerful than this; all other sounds stem from it, just as the pantheon of Hindu gods represents aspects of a single Supreme Being.

On a physical level, chanting *Om* clears the mind, opens energy channels and increases awareness. Spiritually, it can offer a direct

pathway to a state of profound understanding liberated from human failings, such as ignorance, desire and delusion. *Om* includes the three aspects of God in its three audible syllables: "A" stands for Brahma, the Creator; "U" is Vishnu, the Preserver; "M", is Shiva, the Destroyer. Each repetition brings the practitioner into the presence of these Divine principles and into union with the three energies, or *gunas*, which underlie everything in the universe. These syllables also represent the three states of time – past, present and future – and the three states of consciousness – waking, dreaming and sleeping – from which humankind seeks liberation. There is so much meaning bound up in *Om* that it can be meditated on permanently.

Hinduism stirs the depths of the heart and allows room for both communal and individual faith, devotion and sacred knowledge. During festivals and on holy days, such as the Karwachot Festival in Varanasi, northern India, every practising Hindu is expected to bathe in the Ganges before sunrise and engage in *japa yoga*, prayer, recitation of verses and meditation through *mantras*.

SEED *MANTRAS*

These subtle sounds derive from the 50 basic sounds of the sacred Sanskrit language. Although they have no literal meaning, *bija* (seed sounds), form the essence of a *mantra* and are the source of its power. Moreover, seed *mantras* serve as building-blocks for longer *mantras*. Each of the five words set out opposite – a tiny selection from the numerous seed sounds – is very powerful. It centres the person chanting within one of five elements while awakening the particular *chakra* to which each element corresponds and also engaging with one of the five senses.

Ham Corresponds to the energy of the ether and the sense of hearing. Activates and stimulates the throat *chakra*.

Yam Corresponds to the energy of air and the sense of touch. Opens the heart *chakra*, guiding energy up towards the crown, the gateway to bliss.

Ram Corresponds to the energy of fire and the sense of sight. Stimulates the navel *chakra*. Chanting this *mantra* engenders Divine light. Those who die with it on their lips are thought to have achieved *moksha,* or liberation.

Vam Corresponds to the energy of water and the sense of taste. Energises the pelvic *chakra*.

Lam Corresponds to the energy of the earth and the sense of smell. Encourages *prana,* or life force, in the root *chakra* to rise up through the subtle body.

ILLUMINATION BY INVOCATION

"A *mantra* is Divinity encased within a sound structure" states Sri Swami Sivananda (1887–1963 CE) and every deity has a unique *mantra*. Repeating the name of a Divine incarnation, such as *Rama* or *Krishna*, or singing devotional phrases about a particular god, *mahamantra*, concentrates a person in *bhakti* (personal devotion) to this aspect of the Divine, and is a key to transcendence. Because the name and the thing it signifies are essentially the same, the vibrational energy inherent in a Divine name contains something of its essence. Its constant repetition eventually brings the devotee into union with these Divine qualities and the self begins the necessary process of dissolution.

THE *CHAKRAS*

Vocalising any word initiates a physical vibration in the human body. In the Vedic system, certain sounds are linked to the subtle body through the *chakra* system, a pathway of energy centres situated along the *shushumna* energy channel which runs alongside the spine and carries *prana*, or life force, up through the body. *Chakra* means "wheel": each of these seven energy centres vibrates at the frequency of specific sounds which correspond to given *mantras*. Creating the appropriate sound vibration by chanting a *mantra* clears energy blockages in these various *chakras*, enabling the *prana* to flow freely and rise up the subtle energy channel, eventually reaching the crown, or head *chakra*, the gateway to individual self-realisation.

"He who takes refuge in that glorious name knows no pain, no sorrow, no care, no misery. He lives in perfect peace."
SWAMI RAMDAS
(1884–1963 CE)

Japa yoga...

Om

"The sound Om is Brahman...You hear the roar of the ocean from a distance. By following the roar you can reach the ocean. As long as there is the roar, there must also be the ocean. By following the trail of Om you attain Brahman, of which the Word is the symbol."

SRI RAMAKRISHNA (1836–86 CE)

This powerful *mantra* (pronounced "Aah-ooo-mmm") represents the Divine word and is said to be the source of everything that is. A Hindu disciple might set aside 20 minutes each day to chant *Om* with the *mala*, perhaps upon waking and before bed, using similar instructions to those set out here.

Find a calm, quiet, clean place where you can chant each day. Light candles and incense to purify the space and open your mind to prayer. Start by chanting or reciting the sound out loud, working towards a whisper over time, and aiming eventually for silent, internalised, mental repetition (the most potent form of prayer).

1 Find a comfortable, upright position, preferably sitting on the floor. Cross your legs or alternatively assume the lotus or half-lotus position (one foot turned sole-upwards on your opposite thigh). If sitting on the floor is uncomfortable, start by sitting on an upright chair with your back straight and both feet flat on the ground.

2 Hold the *mala* in a *mala* bag (or covered with a clean scarf or a piece of fabric) next to your heart or by your nose. Start at the *meru* bead, then take the first regular bead between the thumb and the middle finger of your right hand. Pause momentarily. Take a deep breath in and feel your diaphragm drop. Breathing out, start to make the sound "Aah".

3 Feel the sound resonate through your body. Take it up from your abdomen into your chest. Shift it into an "Ooo" sound. Bring it up from your throat, into your palate and lips, closing them. Let the sound out as a humming "M". Prolong it to double the length of the previous sounds, letting it drift off until it becomes imperceptible.

4 Move on to the next bead. Repeat the "Aah-ooo-mmm" sound on the exhalation, feeling the energy rising up from your lower abdomen to resonate in your head. If your thoughts wander, tether them back to the sounds.

5 Work through all 108 beads in the same way, rolling each one through your fingers as you make the prolonged sound *Om* as smooth as the pouring of oil. Upon reaching the last bead, work back in the opposite direction, remembering never to pass over the *meru* bead.

6 After finishing the *mantra*, sit in quiet contemplation for a few minutes before returning to the outside world.

Japa yoga...

Reciting Holy Names

This *mantra* invokes the most important names of *Krishna*: *Hare* calls out to the energy of the deity, *Krishna* means "the all-attractive one" and *Rama* signifies supreme bliss. By chanting them, you fill your mind with the presence of the Divine in its preservative aspect.

Fervent devotion to a personal god, or *bhakti* yoga, is one path to self-liberation, for in loving and dwelling upon something, you become inextricably bound to it. Krishna worshippers, for example, surrender every part of themselves to this eighth incarnation of Vishnu, the preservative aspect of Hindu Divinity, whose all-encompassing force seeks to unify and contain opposing and disruptive energies within the universe.

Chant the *mantra* (*see opposite*), the *Mahamantra*, or Mantra of the 16 Names, out loud to come into *dhyana*, or meditation on the attributes of the Divinity. Through intent, love and repetition, this resets the mind to return to an uplifting inner landscape. First of all, start by contemplating an image of the deity.

1 With a conscious intention, repeat the words opposite while rolling the first bead after the larger *meru* or *Krishna* bead between your middle finger and thumb. As you speak, express the qualities of the deity through sound.

2 Repeat the phrase on every bead of the *mala* with intent and devotion, pondering the meaning of the words – the attributes of the Divine – and letting their repetition establish connotations in your mind. When other thoughts threaten to intrude, return to the meaning of the words uttered and to whom they refer.

3 With each word, experience the presence of the Divine permeating the sounds you are uttering. Let the qualities of this aspect of the Divinity pour into you. Link the words with the rhythm of your breath, slow and from your abdomen. Feel them purify you of the residues of anger and cravings.

4 When you reach the last of the *mala* beads, the "summit" of Mount Meru figuratively speaking, work back in the opposite direction. After completing up to 16 repetitions, forwards and backwards, sit quietly with the image of the deity in your heart. Take this memory with you as you re-enter the everyday world.

The Mahamantra

"Hare, Rama;

Hare, Rama;

Rama, Rama;

Hare, Hare;

Hare Krishna;

Hare Krishna;

Krishna, Krishna;

Hare, Hare."

BUDDHIST MALAS

MALA BEADS AND ENLIGHTENMENT
through meditation might be seen as a single concept in
Buddhism. Indeed, the very words "bead" and "Buddha"
derive from the same source – the Sanskrit word *buddh*,
meaning "self-realisation". The ultimate goal of every
practising Buddhist is Buddhahood or *nirvana*: a permanent
and supreme state of bliss, which ends the constant cycle
of birth, death and rebirth. Chanting and contemplation
with prayer beads, or *malas*, is one of the principal routes
to this form of liberation, and has been practised for
centuries in Tibet, China, Japan, Sri Lanka, Korea and
Burma to inspire the devotee to be free from sin, full of
virtue and clean of heart.

LIVING AND CHANTING WITH PRAYER BEADS

The voices of groups of monks chanting together resound from the monasteries of Tibet in a continual murmuring. Appropriately, the Tibetan word for the repetition of a name on the rosary is the same verb used to describe the purring of a cat.

Chanting with a string of 108 prayer beads helps the Buddhist faithful to reach an interior state of supreme reality beyond time and place. In his silent flower sermon, Siddhartha Gautama, the Buddha (563–483 BCE), when asked to shed light on Buddhist laws, merely held up a flower and gazed at it in silence. This silence corresponds to the mystic calm reigning within the supreme state of *nirvana*.

The word derives from the Sanskrit verb *nir-va*, meaning "to blow out", very like a candle. It suggests the extinguishing of

A Buddhist monk in Lhasa, Tibet, meditates as he goes about his daily chores and carries prayer beads with him for this purpose at all times.

ingrained thought and behaviour patterns based on human attachment to sensual pleasures, which bring with them hatred, jealousy, anger and delusion.

Meditating with *mala* beads on this present state of *samsara*, or the cyclical nature of attachment and suffering, enables you to become aware that, as everything you desire and cherish must end, so attachment to it is futile. By confronting this truth, Buddhists come to terms with the transience of all things, gradually learning to surrender the illusion of permanence and attain release from temporal bondage.

THE SUPREME STATE OF BEING
Although most religions venerate God as both a transcendent and immanent being, Buddhists place their emphasis not on God but on a supreme state of being: enlightenment or *nirvana*. In one of the most popular forms of Buddhism practised in China and Japan, this ultimate reality can be reached by chanting the name of *Amitabha Buddha*. Repeated three times to the Buddha,

This free-standing Buddha from Krabi in Thailand, displays all the physical attributes which distinguish "the awakened One" from *bodhisattvas*: half-closed eyes indicating deep meditation, elongated perforated earlobes denoting the renunciation of worldly pleasures and a high protuberance (*ushnisha*) on the head which symbolises omniscience.

dharma (spiritual teachings) and *sangha* (the Buddhist community), the statement or remembrance invoked with the *mala* beads to lead the worshipper towards this state of being translates as "I take refuge in the Buddha of Infinite Light." This invocation, called *Buddha nusmriti* in Sanskrit, *nien-fo* in Chinese and *nembutso* in Japanese, offers deliverance to the individual, as well as serving as a solemn religious sacrament or a means of receiving grace based on unquestioning faith. The saving power of a revealed name, such as *Amitabha Buddha,* enables you to withdraw into the mercy of the Named with surrender and gratitude to tap into a basic serenity, which carries Buddhists towards *Sukhavati,* the Western Paradise of Pure Bliss.

INVOCATORY PRAYER
The central prayer chanted in conjunction with the *mala* in Tibetan Buddhism is *Om Mani Padme Hum* ("O thou jewel in the Lotus, Hail"). The treasure is often interpreted as being the *bodhisattva* Avalokiteshvara, the Buddha of Mercy and Compassion (a *bodhisattva* is an altruistic being who has reached individual enlightenment but delays reaching *nirvana* by returning to earth to help steer others down the ultimate path to self-realisation). Mahayana Buddhism is the only branch of this religion to celebrate *bodhisattvas*.

The lotus on which the Buddha is enthroned is a symbol of his purity and freedom from the faults of cyclic existence. Avalokiteshvara's feminine counterpart is Tara, the dynamic Deity of Compassion, said to have arisen from one of his tears when he cried at how much suffering there is in the world. The figures of Avalokiteshvara and Tara unite masculine and feminine elements, analogous to the Christian prayer *Jesu Maria* and the Hindu invocation *Sita-Rama*. A plant of transformation, the lotus draws nourishment from a pond's muddy bottom to nurture a perfumed blossom. Like the dew-tipped rose of the Roman Catholic tradition, the lotus flower is emblematic of the pure and humble soul opening its petals to receive Divine grace, willing to transcend everyday life and blossom into a state of perpetual bliss.

"It is good to restrain one's mind, uncontrollable, fast moving, and following its own desires as it is. A disciplined mind leads to happiness."
THE BUDDHA
(563–483 BCE)

A Tibetan Buddhist grandmother passes *mala* beads through her fingers while reciting *mantras* (mystical chants) as she takes her grandson to school. The equivalent of this spiritual practice in Christianity is reciting prayers while pausing on the beads of a rosary, a ritual celebrated by spiritual communities as diverse as the Catholics, Greek and Russian Orthodox Christians, Anglicans and Celtic Christians.

PRAYING WITH THE BUDDHIST MALA

Buddhist prayer beads number 108, said in the Japanese Nichiren tradition to be the number of the earthly desires of common mortals. In this belief system, the circlet is known as *jyuzu*, in China *su-zhu,* and *fozhu* and *ojuzu* in the Mahayana Zen tradition, all terms that share the meaning of the words *mala* and rosary – a "garden" or "garland of roses".

The entrance to the 108-bead circle is marked by a large tassel or ribbon and one guru bead, a reminder to the devotee of the importance of having a spiritual teacher. In Sanskrit, *gu* means "dark" and *ru,* "light": the guru leads you out of spiritual darkness and towards enlightenment, or the Light. This is particularly apt with regards to Buddhism, where the Buddha is worshipped less as a god than honoured as a teacher.

The sequence of regular *mala* beads may be interrupted with accent beads of another material, perhaps at bead numbers 21 and 27. The *jyuzu* features four, equally spaced, smaller beads representing the four virtues of the Buddha's life. There are also two larger mother and father beads, both representing the Buddha. Cylindrical, jar-shaped beads acts as receptacles for storing benefits accrued through chanting, and in some traditions signify knowledge or emptiness. A Tibetan *mala*, or *trengwa*, may be adorned with *ghaus* prayer boxes and looks more ornate than its Hindu precursor. "Eternal knots" symbolically acknowledge the interconnectedness of all things.

Two separate cords of 10 beads or discs terminate in thunderbolt pendants, known as *dorjes*, or small bells. These permit the counting of 20 rounds, forwards and backwards, of the 108 beads, making 10,080 repetitions of a single *mantra* theoretically possible in one go!

"Malas
*represent
the Buddha.
Treat them
as you
would
the Buddha."*

REVEREND IDO MIYAHARA (FROM A SPEECH DELIVERED IN 1986 CE)

Japanese *malas* employ even more elaborate ways of counting repetitions to help calculate as many as 36,736 iterations of the same statement. Buddhism often employs an immense number of repetitions to transport the mind beyond the physical act of counting to an original pure and empty state, devoid of distraction.

As *mala* cords fray and break with use, they are invariably restrung. Such physical wear-and-tear serves as a reminder of the Buddha's teachings on life's impermanence and transience and the need to learn non-attachment as a result.

WRIST BEADS

Shorter "quarter" *malas* of 27 beads were traditionally devised for use with prostrate methods of prayer: ideally a *mala* should never touch the ground. In Tibetan Buddhism, cycles of 108 prostrations are performed with wrist *malas* in a practice known as *ngondro*, which acknowledges the sanctity of the three "jewels" of Buddhism – the Buddha himself, the teachings of *dharma,* and *sangha*, or disciples. This practice seeks to purify the human soul from the negative

influence of *karma*, the universal law of cause and effect, which states that doing ill inevitably results in the perpetuation of ill.

SACRED BEADS

Holy seeds are especially revered. *Bodhi malas* are threaded from the seeds of the species of tree under which the Buddha originally attained enlightenment at Bodhgaya in present-day northern India. The seeds of the sacred lotus flower are also highly regarded, representing the potential for spiritual growth under the most inauspicious circumstances. The *rudraksha*-seed *mala* (*see page 63*) is valued for prayers of protection, particularly in Tibet.

Bone malas, such as Sherpa yak bone, prompt the devotee to recall the Buddha's teachings about the impermanence of the world. Most of the holiest *malas* are cut from the skullbones of deceased lamas.

Semi-precious stones, especially in Tibet, are employed to honour deities that have associations with the qualities or colours of the stone: turquoise for

"From meditation springs wisdom."

THE BUDDHA
(563–483 BCE)

金剛悲地蔵

放光王地蔵
元気で発育するよう
子育の楽を司どる

the green deity Tara, red stones for
the medicine Buddha, Sangye Menla.
Remnants of older folk belief are also
common. Amuletic chunks of turquoise
recur in traditional Tibetan *malas* to
ward off danger and bring about
wealth. They may be combined with
beads or discs of the equally talismatic
amber, coral or agate. Associated with
the clarity of spiritual wisdom, the

appearance and the nature of crystal is
such that it is thought to convey,
amplify and project positive energy. It
befits the compassionate contemplative
techniques underlying so much of
Buddhist tolerance, such as *metta*, a
loving-kindness practice in which you
extend love first to yourself and
eventually to all other living beings.

Three statues of
disciples of the
Buddha seated
before sculpted
stone lotus flowers
outside the Daigan-ji
Temple in the state
of Chugoku in Japan.

81

The lotus mantra...

Om Mani Padme Hum

This six-syllable invocation literally translates as "O, thou Jewel in the Lotus, Hail". The most widely used *mantra* in Mahayana Buddhism, it can be found inscribed on rocks, prayer wheels, stupas, *mani* stones, mountain passes, dwelling thresholds and village exits.

The Lotus Mantra incorporates the most powerful and fundamental sound known to both Hindus and Buddhists: *Om.* The chanting and repetition of this sacred word stills the mind, ignites the spirit and consecrates the heart, leading the devotee towards the superior state of being. Uniting mind and heart, it fosters compassion.

Tibetan teachers advise their students to sit like a mountain, stable and immovable, and observe the mind and its thoughts as if it were the infinite sky across which clouds of different shapes and colours pass. You should try to chant for at least 20 minutes every day.

1 Sit in a comfortable position with your spine straight (*see pages 68–69*).

2 Close your eyes and take time to settle mind and body. Feel the breath deep in your abdomen and let each inhalation come naturally.

3 Starting at the *guru* bead, pass each regular bead through your fingers, reciting with it one full *mantra*. Visualise the six syllables as the turning spokes of a wheel of light. Absorb its peace, then project it out to all living beings. Finally, half-open your eyes, becoming conscious of the outside world but still retaining an inner awareness and stillness.

THE JAIN MALA

A Jain frieze from Pangandaran, Java, Indonesia illustrates Jainism's rejection of a God as creator, protector and destroyer of the universe. Its worship rites and spiritual focus are located within a purely human framework instead.

Mahavira, the founder of Jainism, preceded the Buddha by about 100 years. Twenty-three *thirthankaras* (prophet figures) came before the arrival of Mahavira, who recapitulated and systematised the doctrines of all previous *thirthankaras* into what is recognised as Jainism today. The first *thirthankara* is even said to have come at the beginning of time. Like Buddhists, Jains do not worship a creator God, but believe in the potentiality of each soul to become a god in the form of a *siddha*, one

who attains the original state of bliss and so *moksha*, or liberation, from the cycle of rebirth.

THE UNIVERSAL PRAYER

Jain worshippers seek to perfect the soul through *dhyan*, the contemplative stilling of the mind, in which one becomes so absorbed in the true nature of the self and the universe that one is purified and freed from the bondage that is negative *karma*.

The central, fundamental Jain *mantra*, the Navkar Mantra, or Universal Prayer, can be recited upon

mala beads. Instead of mentioning historical founders or saints, it extols the virtues of all spiritually elevated Jains. Worshippers physically bow down to the superior beings who have attained spiritual self-realisation through sacrifice and abstinence, and also honour those who teach the ascendancy and importance of the spiritual over the material.

The Navkar Mantra salutations remind worshippers of the path which all Jains strive for and aspire to. The first paean is not sung to liberated beings, but to *arihantas*, those who show the way because they have found infinite knowledge and no longer suffer attachment, but have yet to die and become *siddhas*. The *mantra* then proceeds to venerate those liberated souls who have attained *moksha,* and pays tribute to *acharyas*, spiritual leaders, and *upadhyayas*, monks with specialist knowledge of the scriptures. The prayer ends by praising all *sadhus* and *sadhvis*, monks and nuns who follow the Jain philosophy and codes of conduct that include an adherence to celibacy, non-violence and a renunciation of wordly pleasures.

THE UNIVERSAL PRAYER

"*Namo Arihantanam*

I bow down to Arihantas

Namo Siddhanam

I bow down to Siddhas

Namo Ayriyanam

I bow down to Acharyas

Namo Uvajjhayanam

I bow down to Upadhyayas

Namo Loe Savva-sahunam

I bow down to Sadhus and Sadhvis

Eso Panch Namokaro

These five salutations

Savva-pavappanasano

Destroy all sins

Manglananch Savvesim

And amongst all that is auspicious

Padhamam Havei Mangalam

This Navkar Mantra is the most auspicious."

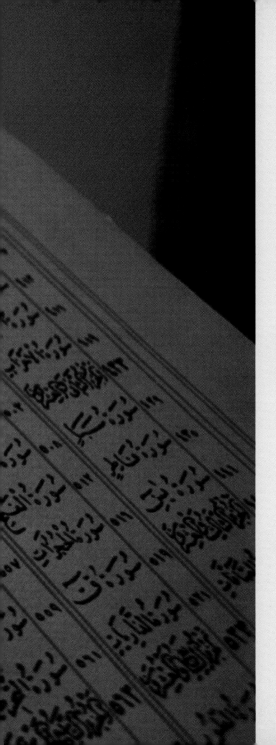

THE MUSLIM TASBIH

"WORSHIP IS THE PILLAR OF RELIGION", proclaimed the Prophet Muhammad ﷺ (570–632 CE). *Salat*, or prayer, is one of the Five Pillars, or essential rites, upholding Islam. Performed five times a day (at dawn, noon, mid-afternoon, sunset and nightfall), prayer punctuates the rhythms of daily life with continual opportunities to come before God in absorbed contemplation. Many Muslims also pray with the *tasbih*, a string of 99 prayer beads; they recite the names of God upon each bead, or repeat exaltations which express their reverence, complete submission and gratitude to the Supreme Being. The power and devotion of each uttered name assists believers in their communion with God.

GLORIFYING GOD

"In the remembrance of Allah do hearts find rest."

THE QUR'AN
(13:28)

The centre of Islam, the sacred sanctuary of the *Kaabah,* is visited by all pilgrims on the *haj,* or pilgrimage, to Mecca in Saudi Arabia. The Qur'an states that the lower the prostration, the closer one comes into the presence of the Divine. Communal prayer is regarded as a more powerful means of communing with God than private supplication alone.

The word *tasbih* derives from the Arabic root s-b-h which means "to glorify". Each of this rosary's 99 beads represents one of the names, or attributes, of God. Muslims believe that God's Divine qualities combine in various proportions to create the universe around us, and that all the names are contained in the Name, or word *Allah* – interestingly, a neuter word in the Arabic language. Hence by repeating this Name during invocation, a sacred rite known as *dhikr* or remembrance, the worshipper participates in the manifestation of creation. Muslims

A 12th-century Mogul miniature painting of a saintly Muslim from India.

usually complete each of the five daily prayers by repeating the following phrases 99 times and counting out each repetition on the *tasbih* or on the fingers: *Subhana'llah* (Glory be to God); *Alhamdulillah* (All Praise is due to God); *Allahu akhbar* (God is most Great).

THE ASCENSION

The Prophet Muhammad ﷺ (570–632 CE) likened worship to a ladder, a route by which humankind might ascend into the presence of God. Writing about the benefits of worship, the 18th-century Mogul mystical savant, Shah Waliullah of Delhi (1703–61 CE), spoke of the state of prayer as a type of absorption during which the soul is taken over by the Divine Presence and one sees and feels that which "the human tongue is incapable of describing". He explained that the physical positions adopted by Muslims during prayer are a type of quest, an attempt to reengage with an ecstatic "state of light". In bowing his or her forehead to the ground, a Muslim attempts to submit will and being before the Creator. Prostration is a powerful physical symbol reflecting human lowliness before the majesty of God. As the Qur'an clearly states, "Bow down and draw near" (96:19). Repeated standing, bowing and prostration, and the reiterated sacred formulae of the daily services, purify body and heart. The believer gradually draws closer to God and thus is able to approach the Divine realm by repeating verses revealed by God directly through the Prophet Muhammad ﷺ.

> *"...one is sometimes transported, quick as lightning, to the Holy Precincts (of the Divine Presence), and finds one's self attached...to the threshold of God."*
>
> SHAH WALIULLAH OF DELHI (1703–61 CE)

GLORIFYING GOD

89

THE TASBIH

"Repeat the Tasbih a hundred times, and a thousand virtues shall be recorded by God for you, 10 virtuous deeds for each repetition."
THE PROPHET MUHAMMAD ﷺ (570–632 CE)

Although the s-b-h root within *tasbih* refers to glorification, s-b-h bears an etymological reference to "finger", as in praying with beads. Usually totalling 99 beads, one for each of the names, or attributes, of God, some sets comprise only 33 but are prayed upon three times over during worship. The 100th name, the Name of the Essence, is found in Paradise.

This Muslim rosary is divided into three equal sections, separated by a tassel or by accent beads of a different colour or shape to the regular beads. A single longer bead holds all the beads in place and additional tassels, threaded with 10 counter beads each, enable greater repetitions of prayers. The tassel at the entrance to the *tasbih* is known as *El-shaheed* ("the witness"); the longer bead is the "A" or *Alif*, the source of knowledge and awareness.

GIFTS OF CREATION

Although the beads themselves can be created from virtually any material, those made from precious stones, terracotta or various types of wood, such as sandalwood, rose or olive, are most commonly used to offer a constant reminder of and connection with God's creation. Terracotta beads gain in sacredness if rolled out of clay obtained from Mecca, the spiritual heart of the Muslim world. Lapis lazuli from Afghanistan is the more traditional choice for beads, and carnelian is a stone renowned for having a special connection with the Prophet Muhammad ﷺ, who reputedly wore an inscribed carnelian ring and preached that whoever wore this type of stone would be blessed. Silver is also considered a particularly suitable metal to incorporate in prayer beads.

THE UNITY OF THE SPHERE

Medieval Islamic mathematicians revived and refined the work of early Greek scientists after the decline of Western learning following the 3rd century CE, laying down the basic foundations for most of the mathematical knowledge later used in Renaissance Europe. Their laws of geometry proposed that all shapes and forms derive from that of the sphere. These advances were influential in the development of Islamic art, which excels at elaborately abstract geometric patterns based on the divisions of the circle; all of them hint at the infinite, which goes on *ad infinitum*. The beads and the shape of the *tasbih* itself resonate with this prime cosmological symbol. The string of beads also mirrors the Islamic arabesque style in which complex arrangements of smaller geometric forms relate to the larger whole, such as in fractal geometry.

The *tasbih* may be used at will after canonical prayers, regardless of place: inside a mosque, a private house, a park or a street corner in Bukhara, Uzbekistan.

Praying with the tasbih...

Reciting God's 99 Names

Including the name *Al-'Ali* (The Most High), God has 99 most "beautiful names" which the Prophet Muhammad ﷺ is said to have encouraged his followers to recite while counting beads on the *tasbih*.

The Prophet Muhammad ﷺ declared, "Clothe yourself with the excellent qualities of God Most High…God has nine and ninety virtues: whosoever puts on one of them will surely enter the Garden [Heaven]." It is also enough simply to recite the name *Allah*, which contains all 99 names or Divine qualities. Each name can also easily become a prayer in itself: replace the prefix with *Yaa*, a salutation to that name, and repeat the phrase 33 times, meditating on the qualities of the Name with intent and humility to invoke its blessings. When someone is ill, for example, it is common practice for Muslims to gather together to recite the prayer *Yaa Latif* (O Most Gentle One).

1 Begin by holding the first bead and say *La ilaha illallah* (There is no god but God). Then, moving the beads between the fingers, recite one of the 99 names (*see opposite*) on each individual bead.

2 After reciting the last name on the final bead, say *Al-hamdu lillahi rabbil 'alamin* (Praise be to God, Lord of the worlds).

The 99 Names of God

"Ar-Rahman, the Beneficent; Ar-Rahim, the Merciful; Al-Malik, the Eternal Lord; Al-Quddus, the Most Sacred; As-Salam, the Embodiment of Peace; Al-Mu'min, the Infuser of Faith; Al-Muhaymin, the Preserver of Safety; Al-'Aziz, the Mighty One; Al-Jabbar, the Omnipotent One; Al-Mutakabbir, the Dominant One; Al-Khaliq, the Creator; Al-Bari', the Evolver; Al-Musawwir, the Flawless Shaper; Al-Ghaffar, the Great Forgiver; Al-Qahhar, the All-Prevailing One; Al-Wahhab, the Supreme Bestower; Ar-Razzaq, the Total Provider; Al-Fattah, the Supreme Solver; Al-'Alim, the All-Knowing One; Al-Qabid, the Restricting One; Al-Basit, the Extender; Al-Khafid, the Reducer; Ar-Rafi', the Elevating One; Al-Mu'izz, the Honourer-Bestower; Al-Muzill, the Abaser; As-Sami', the All-Hearer; Al-Basir, the All-Noticing; Al-Hakam, the Impartial Judge; Al-'Adl, the Embodiment of Justice; Al-Latif, the Knower of Subtleties; Al-Khabir, the All-Aware One; Al-Halim, the Clement One; Al-'Azim, the Magnificent One; Al-Ghafur, the Great Forgiver; Ash-Shakur, the Acknowledging One; Al-'Ali, the Sublime One; Al-Kabir, the Great One; Al-Hafiz, the Guarding One; Al-Muqit, the Sustaining One; Al-Hasib, the Reckoning One; Aj-Jalil, the Majestic One; Al-Karim, the Bountiful One; Ar-Raqib, the Watchful One; Al-Mujib, the Responding One; Al-Wasi', the All-Pervading One; Al-Hakim, the Discreet One; Al-Wadud, the Loving One; Al-Majid, the Glorious One; Al-Ba'ith, the Infuser of New Life; Ash-Shahid, the All-Observing Witness; Al-Haqq, the Embodiment of Truth; Al-Wakil, the Universal Trustee; Al-Qawi, the Strong One; Al-Matin, the Firm One; Al-Wali, the Protecting Associate; Al-Hamid, the Sole-Laudable One; Al-Muhsi, the All-Enumerating One; Al-Mubdi', the Originator; Al-Mu'id, the Restorer; Al-Muhyi, the Maintainer of Life; Al-Mumit, the Inflictor of Death; Al-Hayy, the Eternally Living One; Al-Qayyum, the Self-Subsisting One; Al-Wajid, the Pointing One; Al-Majid, the All-Noble One; Al-Wahid, the Only One; Al-Ahad, the Sole One; As-Samad, the Supreme Provider; Al-Qadir, the Omnipotent One; Al-Muqtadir, the All-Authoritative One; Al-Muqaddim, the Expediting One; Al-Mu'akhkhir, the Procrastinator; Al-Awwal, the Very First; Al-Akhir, the Infinite Last One; Az-Zahir, the Perceptible; Al-Batin, the Imperceptible; Al-Wali, the Holder of Supreme Authority; Al-Muta'ali, the Extremely Exalted One; Al-Barr, the Fountainhead of Truth; At-Tawwab, the Ever-Acceptor of Repentance; Al-Muntaqim, the Retaliator; Al-'Afuw, the Supreme Pardoner; Ar-Ra'uf, the Benign One; Malik-ul-Mulk, the Eternal Possessor of Sovereignty; Dhul-Jalali-wal-Ikram, the Possessor of Majesty and Reverence; Al-Muqsit, the Just One; Aj-Jami', the Assembler of Scattered Creations; Al-Ghani, the Self-Sufficient One; Al-Mughni, the Bestower of Sufficiency; Al-Mani', the Preventor; Ad-Daarr, the Distressor; An-Nafi', the Bestower of Benefits; An-Nur, the Prime Light; Al-Hadi, the Provider of Guidance; Al-Badi', the Unique One; Al-Baqi, the Ever Surviving One; Al-Warith, the Eternal Inheritor; Ar-Rashid, the Guide to the Path of Rectitude; As-Sabur, the Extensively Enduring One."

SUFI MYSTICISM

The Sufi *sheikh,* or master (an elder empty of all but God), guides the seeker in prayers and invocations to facilitate a deeper spirituality, aimed at eliminating the influence of the ego. Through such subtle restraint, aspirants experience the Divine as the all-pervading reality.

Sufism is an inner or esoteric dimension of Islam for those both with the aptitude or the desire to accelerate the spiritual process. A seeker becomes the disciple of a master, or *sheikh* (the Arabic word for an elderly, wise man). These sages can trace their lineage back to the Prophet Muhammad ﷺ and give voluntary guidance to devout Muslims in the course of sanctification or the re-gaining of the *fitra,* humankind's pure, primordial nature.

The disciple of a Sufi master is ever careful and willing to comply with all the obligatory prayers, fasts, charity and pilgrimages required of ordinary, practising Muslims. In addition to these mandatory activities, using the *tasbih* two or three times daily is also expected with the aim of attaining in the heart a permanent state of remembrance of God. Daily prayer rituals with the *tasbih* help the seeker to curb the influence of the ego by focusing the concentration on strengthening both heart and mind on God. Disciples are also requested to

perform regular retreats, or *khalwas,* and attend devotional gatherings held by their spiritual brotherhood.

CONSTANT AWARENESS
The rite of *dhikr* (remembrance of God by repetition of the Divine Name and other formulae) centres the Sufi seeker within to reside in God's presence. Different forms of *dhikr* suit specific occasions and times of day (before sleep, on waking, at midday, after the five daily prayers), and may be accompanied by meditation on verses from the Qur'an. *Dhikr* involves reciting God's 99 names or, with the permission of a *sheikh,* the word *Allah,* while using the *tasbih* so that the Divine quality within each Name induces a God-absorbed spiritual state. Other phrases used in repetitions include: *La ilaha illallah* (There is no god but God); *Subhana'llah* (Glory be to God); *Alhamdulillah* (All Praise is due to God); *Allahu akhbar* (God is most Great); and *Astaghfiru llah* (May God forgive me).

During invocation, a Sufi disciple may focus on his heartbeat, so that all but God disappears. Every breath should be invested with an awareness of the Divine: it is even intimated that the collective sound of the inhalations and exhalations of all living beings forms the name of God. Other techniques, such as those used by the Mevlevi "whirling dervishes" of Turkey, incorporate rhythmic movements: those to the right represent the body and the world; those to the left symbolise the heart.

There are three stages of *dhikr*: firstly, recitations are purely verbal; secondly, heart and tongue unite to open the seeker's heart through the Supreme Name; finally, *La ilaha illallah* is attained, where there is no reality except God. The ultimate achievement is *fana fi Allah* (the extinction of the self in God).

Dervish orders in Turkey, Albania, Egypt, Syria, Tunisia and Ethiopia may use dance and music in *dhikr* to bridge the gap between man and creator. Dervishes renounce the material world in favour of God.

Praying with the tasbih...
The Sufi Way

In the Islamic mystical path, a disciple performs *wird* – a special prayer designated by a master – on the *tasbih* usually two or three times a day. He or she practises the death of the ego and the re-formation of the soul to its original pure nature which leads to a re-union with God.

Wird shares the same Arabic etymological root as *ward* ("rose") and *wardiya* ("rosary"). W-r-d also signifies "to enter", "to travel to" or "to blossom into". Here, we compare the journey of the Sufi traveller with the path a Christian takes within the sacred rite of Holy Communion.

Both Muslims and Christians participate in an emptying of the self, a "death" of all things that are unholy or unfavourable within themselves. This stage of internal purification can be compared to the death St John of the Cross (1542–91 CE) described thus: "Die before you die". After this emptying or "death", come reformation and resurrection which, according to the Christian mystic Meister Eckhart (*c.* 1260–1328 CE), leads to a union with the Godhead to grant eternal life.

1 The first stage involves an act of repentance, essentially an emptying away of the lower self, or *nafs*. A Muslim attempting to re-establish his or her originally pure nature will repeat *Astagfir Allah* (May God forgive me) 99 times. This declaration of faith is uttered by the aspirant with the heartfelt intention of sincerely desiring to change, and it is known as *tawbah,* or turning. The equivalent Christian gesture would be the devotee praying *Kyrie eleison* (Lord have mercy, Christ have mercy), before reaching the altar to receive the Sacraments during Holy Communion.

2 In the second stage of praying with the *tasbih,* the Muslim worshipper pauses on each bead and repeats *Allahumma salli ala sayyidna Muhammad* ﷺ (Blessings and praises upon Prophet Muhammad ﷺ), with the intention of striving to regain the *fitra,* or condition of True Man or Woman. In Christianity, a parallel may be drawn with waiting to receive the sacramental bread and wine, understood, both symbolically and literally, to be the body and the blood of Christ. When the word of God, or *logos,* is taken within the aspirant's own emptiness, he or she re-gains a Christ-like nature, practising a re-formation of the self.

3 In the final stage, both Muslims and Christians are intent on uniting with or returning to the Divine Source of all Being. The Muslim repeats *La ilaha illallah* (There is no god but God) on the rosary 99 times, attesting to the absence of anything that is not God – neither the vessel full of itself nor the empty vessel filled with True Man or Woman. In Christianity, the comparative moment comes when the worshipper, having received the Sacraments, kneels before the altar, and his or her soul rises pure to God through the medium of the Holy Spirit. Both Christians and Muslims jointly strive to return to the One, the source of all creation.

NATIVE AMERICAN BEADS

FOR MANY INDIGENOUS PEOPLES OF the Americas, such as the Huichol in Mexico, the Ojibwe in Canada, and the Iroquois in the United States, the act of beading, like reciting the rosary, is a reverential, repetitive therefore meditative ritual, which provides a way of experiencing the "heartbeat of creation" while opening a conduit to the Divine realm. It represents a way of handing down vital myths – the lifeblood of a community – just as the rosary instils set prayers in the mind of a congregation. The beads, considered to be gifts from God, have been exchanged in trade, strung to record songs and treaties, used to mark rites of passage and to celebrate religious ceremonies for over 8,000 years.

DANCING WITH THE SPIRIT WORLD

A huge diversity exists within the spiritual practices of the native peoples of North America: each grouping has its own unique oral tradition, teachings, mythology, cosmogony and lineage. For many tribes, centuries of bloodshed, repression and forcible conversion to Christianity by missionaries and settlers have severed the oral traditions by which religious beliefs were handed down across generations of tribespeople to contribute to a distinct cultural heritage. Only with the passing of the Freedom of Religion Act (1978) were Native Americans no longer forced to serve a jail term of up to 30 years for the criminal offence of practising some aspects of indigenous spirituality.

What strongly emerges from the 250 disparate groups which comprise the Native American nation in the 21st century is the sense of a spiritual life so rich that it completely interconnects with and is assimilated within the everyday secular world. Many tribes share the notion of a single-creator God, called *Wakan-Tanka* (the Great Spirit) by the Lakota, which manifests in all things and is embodied in – as well as embodies – every part of the universe. Every act subsequently becomes a ritual of reverence for and unification with this primordial force. When the Divine is identifiable in all the natural elements – the sun, the wind, the light, the dark, water, earth, man and woman – life itself becomes a continual prayer: hunting, harvesting, even the mundane ritual of getting dressed, take on the function of a bridge or a dance between the physical and the spirit worlds.

FORMS OF PRAYER

The vision quest is a widespread prayer rite which takes the form of solitary retreat in the wilderness. Through fasting and contemplation, the seeker approaches the spirit world and is rewarded with spiritual power or insight. Another form of prayer ceremony, the sweat lodge, purifies the whole person by preparing him or her to encounter God in nakedness. With the pipe, the sacred object through which Native

> *"The heart is a sanctuary at the centre of which there is a little space, wherein the Great Spirit dwells, and this is the Eye...by which He sees all things and through which we can see Him."*
>
> BLACK ELK (1863–1950 CE), OGALA-DAKOTA HOLY MAN

Americans most often engage in daily devotion, tobacco transmogrifies into smoke and carries prayers on the winds to the Great Spirit. Repeating a sacred name while smoking the pipe impresses every part of a person's being with the presence of the Divine. The pipe serves as a vivid reminder of the need for constant prayer and offers a channel for the power of the creator to express itself: the stem acts as a passage for the sacred breath and the bowl represents the heart ignited by the spark of the Divine.

Beading is a vital component of prayer ceremonies and enhances the ritual of the pipe. Bandolier "doctor" bags, beaded by prayerful women, are worn by revered elders during healing and initiation rites and heighten spirituality. Designs incorporate signs from visions, and meaningful cosmological symbols, patterns and colours, such as the Iroquois celestial tree. Ceremonial pipes may be inlaid with glass beads by tribes, such as the Senecca Iroquois, in remembrance of God's all-seeing eye.

PRAYING WITH THE PIPE

In the Crow tribal tradition, believers are urged to usher in and seal each living day by offering prayers to God through the ceremonial pipe. Once lit, the pipe is raised in honour of *Acbadadea*, Maker of All Things, angled down towards Mother Earth, then ritualistically spun in the four directions of the winds and the Medicine Fathers (animals and objects in nature through which blessings and gifts from God are received). When offering prayers with smoke, one calls on one's own Medicine Fathers and personal prayers are offered before the tobacco is completely smoked. As tobacco represents creation to the Lakota, the act of smoking literally "absorbs" the worshipper into the contents of the universe. The Teton–Dakota ritual of the Raising of the Pipe to each of the directions opens up the gates through which Divine essence can flow through the pipe into the smoker and out again to bless everything in the universe.

SACRED BEADING

Traditionally, the Divine was believed to be embedded in every piece of native beadwork in the form of holy motifs, in the natural world depicted and in the beaders' sacred dedication to the task. Beading by loom or appliqué was considered a blessed undertaking in which technical perfection was pursued alongside focused mindfulness. Women accepted the work as a sacred token or a vow in the heart, and a particular piece would come to be regarded as a form of prayer for the person it was made to honour. As they worked, beaders were urged to think good thoughts, contemplate nature and revere the tiny beads as offerings from the spirit world: originally arriving in the form of stone, bone, horn, quill and shell, they literally came from the earth and water.

Indigenous beaders embraced the arrival of tiny glass rocailles and bugles following Columbus' first offerings to the Bahamian Arawak Indians in 1492. Synthetic beads were jointly valued for their colour and symbolic appearance. The hard transparency and water-like sheen of glass recalled crystal, considered a powerful lens with which to view the soul and tap into the spirit world. Several words used by the Algonquian for glass, mirrors and metal, for example, link directly with terms for seeing and the soul. Interestingly, the Ontario Ojibwe's Divine name – *Manito* – translates as "mirror".

The tiny glass beads thought to resemble seeds or berries became favourites. Anishnabe beaders referred to them as *manidoominens*, gift of the Great Spirit, or *Manidoo*. *Miinens* also signifies the fruit of the hawthorn tree, considered to be sacred. When Indians first encountered Christianity, different styles of beadwork and varying notions of spirituality collided. Ursuline nuns found themselves teaching European embroidery techniques to 18th-century Ojibwe girls. In the amalgamation of contrasting cultures which ensued as the two traditions merged, indigenous converts relayed the ancient symbolic significance of the hawthorn to their tribe, while being taught that those same branches formed Christ's crown of thorns.

STORY BEADS

Beads were used as a means of recording information. Wampum chains – belts of the most highly revered beads made of purple or white shell tubes – marked treaties and documented songs and ceremonies. Storytelling accompanied community beading sessions, passing on essential truths and mythology. Story strings – circlets of beads carved into animals and figures – are said to have been used for tale-telling. Some say this tradition derived from Native American encounters with missionaries' rosaries, although story rings resemble the amuletic necklaces of the Tairona people of Columbia (800–1500 CE).

For Mexico's Huichol Indians today, beading still codifies the spiritual beliefs and history of an ancient oral society, so that the act of beading continues to be inseparable from that of praying and connecting with the spiritual realm.

In the Americas, the act of beading, such as that practised by the Huichol Indians of Mexico and the American Southwest, is as powerfully prayerful as the sacred object it creates. Symbolic colours, forms and materials, often received in visions, weave the spirit world into physical objects, such as the beaded *jicara* prayer bowls, which become repositories for a belief in the interconnectedness of all things. As the seeds originally used in the beading ripen into a nourishing foodstuff, so the beads fixed to the bowl in sacred patterns will bring prayers to fruition.

AMULETS AND MEDITATION

THROUGHOUT HISTORY, HUMANKIND has strung, counted and worn beads not only as a form of religious devotion, but as an act of meditation to focus the mind, help solve problems and dispel fear by drawing on the archetypal protective powers of beads. Whether they be pebbles pierced by the pounding of the sea, or plastic worry beads hanging from car rearview mirrors, these objects help people to detach from life's everyday difficulties by calming the mind. People today wear power beads, adapted from the Buddhist wrist-*mala* tradition, using them to chant good-fortune or healing *mantras,* while others borrow practices from the Catholic rosary tradition to honour Pagan deities, such as the goddess.

WORRY BEADS

(see pages 38–39)

Komboloi, Greek worry beads, derive their name from the word *kombos*, meaning "a number of knots" and *loi*, "a group that stays together". Although not religious objects *per se*, the word *komboloi* is too close to one of the prayer-rope terms of the Greek Orthodox tradition – *kombologion* (*see pages 38–39*) – for there to be no historical connection. Some historians suggest that the quotidian use of beads in Greece can be traced back to 400 years of Turkish rule after the fall of Constantinople in 1453. Like shorter *tasbih* prayer beads used by Muslim invaders, worry beads sometimes total 33, although 16–20 are generally more common numbers. Plastic or amber are the favoured materials. Amber beads have been worn for

their protective powers throughout the world since Paleolithic times: the resin is esteemed for its electrical charge and warmth to the touch. The generally large beads are adorned with tassels and saints' medals – most commonly, that of St Christopher – or lucky talismans, including dice and blue-glass eye beads.

Throughout the Greek isles, people find themselves counting worry beads through the fingers and twirling them around their hands as they go about their daily business, not for prayer, but as a form of secular mental focus, a way of steadying the mind by occupying the body with rhythm, sound and texture. The practice of this relaxing habit, like its religious counterpart, results in a sense of calm and well-being. Once the provenance of

"May all good things come to you.

May nothing whatsoever harm you."

TRADITIONAL
BLESSING

men alone, worry beads are now increasingly popular with women as growing numbers seek to tackle and overcome stress within the workplace. Some people claim that worry beads have helped them to give up unhealthy habits, such as smoking or overeating, by offering effective means of stress-relief and distractions from problems.

Elsewhere, religious prayer beads became secularized. The Buddhist *mala* came to be handled in a non-religious manner, similar to worry beads, in Manchurian China (1644–1912 CE). Period paintings show court officials using the *mala* as an abacus. The emperor's rosary, originally made of pearls, betrays the origins of the modern-day pearl necklace.

EYE BEADS

Common to many cultures, talismanic eye beads, known as *matia* in Greece, form part of sets of worry beads, or worry knots. Their influence is so ubiquitous that some of the crucifixes on sacred Greek Orthodox prayer beads actually incorporate *matia* beads, too. Eye beads are invariably cobalt blue in colour and made of glass. Some have an eye motif created from layers of white and yellow glass, but a single blue bead is enough to signify an eye bead, as may be seen in Middle Eastern countries, Greece and India. Such beads are believed to ward off the malevolent powers of the evil-eye by distracting it away from a person's own eyes with its glassy reflection. They are commonly strung around the necks of infants and young children for their protective powers.

ADAPTING TRADITIONS

The state of spiritual mindfulness sought by religious devotees when counting prayer repetitions using beads is becoming increasingly attractive to generations with no traditional belief systems which prescribe meditation to still the mind. Power beads – 9, 21 or 27 usually semi-precious stones worn around the wrist like the Buddhist wrist-*mala* – are fingered to relieve stress rather like Greek worry beads. Users pick and mix these semi-precious stones guided by global folk beliefs which recount tales of their ability to heal and bring good luck. Others have adapted the Catholic rosary as a way of honouring a personal selection of deities from pagan religion, such as the goddess or the horned god.

HEALING PROPERTIES

Formed over millions of years from pressure exerted by the earth's crust, semi-precious stones retain the primal colours of nature and so are honoured across cultures for aligning the wearer with the elements. In doing so they are said to rebalance mind, body and spirit and bring luck. Rock crystal, for example, is considered the most

powerful stone by native peoples in places as diverse as Tibet, Australia and the Americas. It has been used as a vehicle to access other worlds and, like colour and sound, is believed to emit an energy charge potent enough to purify and clear energy blockages in the body *chakras* (*see pages 66–67*).

Specific beads are selected for meditation based on the qualities that a particular stone and its respective colour conveys, or to match an astrological birth chart. Blue stones, for instance, such as lapis lazuli and aquamarine, are considered to be cleansing and ward off danger. Yellow-red stones, such as garnet and carnelian, are thought to purify and fire the heart and represent female energy.

Power bracelets, said to be invested with healing energy through the mindfulness involved in their making, are often supplied with affirmations or personal *mantras* to be repeated with breath meditations. Power beads can also be used for divination: choose a bead at random, then pass each remaining bead through your fingers, replying "yes" or "no" to the question you have asked until you reach the final answer at the large bead. People who use worry and

power beads attest to their capacity to
stimulate acupoints on the hand, thus
enhancing attributes, such as vitality,
wisdom and intuition. Historically, points
on the fingers have always been stimulated
through counting, whether for prayers or to
tally sums. In the Far and Middle East, the
pious, shopkeepers and schoolchildren alike
count on the actual creases of their fingers.

WORSHIPPING THE GODDESS
Rosary beads are being strung to match an
increasingly eclectic range of beliefs. Woven
into the traditional 150-bead template of
the Catholic rosary are talismans and
pendants representing saints, angels and other
Divine symbols. Goddess rosaries contain
beads and charms with gloriously enlarged
breasts and thighs to celebrate femininity.
Different colours are used in a rosary to
honour the goddess in her three aspects –
white for the maiden, red for the mother
and black for the crone. Groups of 13 beads
represent the moons of the year, with a
larger silver gateway bead for the full moon.

Beads hanging inside vehicles from rearview mirrors
can be seen to have a similar function as the strings
tied to donkeys and camels, placed there to protect
their owner's livelihood and ward off the evil-eye.

INDEX

Abba Cronius 40
Abbot Thomas Keating 42
Acupoints in fingers 108
Algonquian tribe, North
    America 102
Amethyst beads 25
Angel Gabriel 20
Anglican prayer bead rope 42
Anglican Prayer Movement
Anishnabe tribe, North
    America 102
Annunciation 20
Apostle John 45
Apostle's Creed 26, 31
Arawak Indians 102
Ashkenazic Jewish tradition 55
Ave (Hail Mary) beads 22-23

Batim boxes 48-50, 54-55
Beading, North American
    101-103
Bhakti yoga 67, 70
Black Elk 101
Bodhisattva 77
Bone *malas* 80
Book of Common Prayer, The 42
Brahma 60, 63, 65
Breathing in prayer/breath
    meditations 40-41, 69, 95,
    108
Brigittine rosary 23
Buddha, The 10, 15, 75, 77,
    79-81

Buddha of Mercy and
    Compassion 77
Buddha (statue) 14, 76
Buddhism
    chant 17, 75
    Mahayana 77, 82
    malas 75-82, 107
    Tantric 77
Burnett, Frances Hodgson 15

Celtic Christianity 45
Celtic cross 45
Centering Prayer Movement 42
Chakras 66-67, 108
Chanting 17, 34, 66-67, 75
Om 64-65, 68-69
Circle imagery 12, 15, 45, 62,
    91
Columbus 102
Coral beads 25
Crow tribe, North America 101
Crown of Our Lady rosary 23
Crown of Our Lord rosary 23
Crucifix 23, 39
Crucifixion 23, 39, 42

Daigan-ji Temple, Japan 81
Dervish orders 94

Eastern Orthodox Church 34
Eye beads 107

Fatima Prayer 31
Fingers, acupoints in 108
Freedom of Religion Act 100

Garden imagery 10-12, 14-15,
    62, 79
Garden of Eden 10, 15, 20
Gethsemane 23
Glorious Mysteries
    (The Redemption) 28
Glory Be (prayer) 27
Great Urn Festival, India 60
Gul medallions 10
Guru 64, 77

Hail Mary beads 22-23
Hail Mary (prayer) 27
Hail, Holy Queen (prayer) 30
Hesychia (Hesychast method)
    33, 37
Hindu prayer 60
Holy Communion 96-97
Huichol tribe, Mexico 99, 103

Ibn Arabi 16
Invocation 12, 15-16, 34, 42,
    59, 64, 67, 77, 94-95
Iroquois tribe, North America
    99, 101
Islam 87-97

Jain *mantra* 84
Jainism 84-85
Japanese *Nichiren* tradition 79
Jerusalem 23
Jesus Christ 20, 25, 28, 34,
    42, 45
Jesus prayer 34, 37, 40-41, 43
Joyful Mysteries
    (The Creation) 28
Julian of Norwich 42

Karma 80, 84
Karwachot Festival, India 64
King Solomon 47
Krishna 70
Khumba Mela *see* Great Urn
    Festival

Lakota tribe, North America
    100
Lhasa, Tibet 75
Lotus flower 77
Lotus *Mantra* 17, 82

Madonna of the Garden, The
    10
Mahamantra 70-71
Mahayana Buddhism 77, 79, 82
Malas,
    bone 80
    Buddhist 75-82

Hindu 59-63,
seed 80
semi-precious stones 80-81
Mantra(s) 60, 64
invocations of deities 64,
70
Jain 84
Lotus 17, 82
Mahamantra 70-71
Navkar 85-86
Om 64, 82
seed 64, 66
Meditation 75
Meister Eckhart 96
Mevlevi dervishes 94
Mezzuzah parchments 54
Montefeltro altarpiece 25
Mount Athos 33
Mount Meru 71
Mount of Olives 23
Muslim faith 88

Native American peoples
100-103
Navkar Mantra 85-86
Naxos, Greece 33, 35
Nirvana 73, 75
Numerology in Judaism 54

Ojibwe tribe, Canada 99,
102
Olive-wood beads 23
Om mani padme hum 17, 77,
82

Orthodox cross 39
Our Father (prayer) 27

Pangandaran, Java, Indonesia
84
Paradise 10, 20
Paternoster 22
Pearl beads 25
Persian carpets 10
Philokalia 17
Piero della Francesca 25
Pope John Paul II 25
Prana 67
Prayer rope 34, 37-38, 40
Prayers
Anglican 42-43
Buddhist 77-82
Celtic Christian 45
Hindu 60, 62
Jain 84-85
Judaic practice 48-57
Muslim 88-93
Native American 100-103
Orthodox 34-41
Roman Catholic 20,
22-23, 26-31
Prophet Muhammad 87,
89-90, 92, 94, 97

Qur'an, The 88-89

Retzuos straps 49-50, 53-55
Reverend Ido Miyahara 79

Rosary 10-13, 20-37
Muslim 87, 90-96
Rosary *Upanishad* 60, 63
Rose
petal beads 12-13, 23
symbol of 10
Ruby beads 63
Russian Orthodox Church 37

Sadhana (Hindu prayer) 60
Sangye Menla 81
Sapphire beads 25
Secret Garden, The 15
Seed *malas* 80
Semi-precious stones 80-81,
108
Sephardic Jewish tradition 55
Shah Waliullah of Delhi 89
Shamrock 45
Shiva 63, 65
Siddha(s) 84-85
Siddhartha Gautama *see* Buddha
Sorrowful Mysteries
(The Fall) 28
Sri Ramakrishna 68
Sri Ramana Maharshi 63
Sri Swami Sivananda 67
St Augustine 12, 15, 20
St Brigid's cross 45
St Christopher 106
St Gregory of Sinai 37
St Hildegard 25
St Isaac the Syrian 34
St Patrick 45
St Paul 34

St Theresa of Avila 12
Stefano da Verona 10
Stillness, finding 15-16, 60
Sufism 94
Swami Ramdas 64, 67

Tairona people, Columbia
103
Tantric Buddhism 77
Tara, Deity of Compassion
77, 80
Tasbih 87, 90-96, 106
Tefillin 48-50, 53-57
Topaz beads 25
Torah 48-50, 54

Universal Prayer 84
Upanishads 60, 63

Vedic tradition 60, 64, 67
Virgin Mary 10, 20, 22-23,
28, 45
Vishnu 62-63, 65, 70

Wakan-Tanka 100
Way of A Pilgrim, The 37
Western Paradise of Pure Bliss
77
Wood beads 63
Worry beads 106
Wrist beads 80, 108

ACKNOWLEDGEMENTS

Carroll & Brown Limited would like to thank:
Production manager Karol Davies
Production controller Nigel Reed
Computer management Paul Stradling
Picture researcher Sandra Schneider
Indexer Madeline Weston

Text for chapters 1–6 is based on Gray Henry's video *Beads of Faith* (© Fons Vitae 2000), Fons Vitae, 49 Mockingbird Valley Drive, Louisville, KY 40207, USA; www.fonsvitae.com.

I sincerely hope that the images and passages from my video, *Beads of Faith*, which have served as the inspiration for this effort with Susannah Marriott, will truly support any person desiring to deepen his or her own understanding of one of the most essential spiritual tools and methodologies to grace humankind. For me, the invocation upon my rosary has served as "a rope thrown by God to a drowning man" through such severe trials as paralysis. My rosary also recalls the joyous heights and blessings found in nature, beloved friends and sacred sanctuaries. With these precious beads may we all draw closer to God's divine presence, with hearts purified.

Virginia Gray Henry

Susannah Marriott would like to dedicate this book to her daughters, Olive and Stella, and thank Gray for her inspiration and insight. Heartfelt thanks to: the Most Reverend Dr Rowan Williams, Archbishop of Wales and Bishop of Monmouth; William Stoddart; Bishop Kallistos Ware; Rama Coomaraswamy; Michael Fitzgerald; Tenzin Bob Thurman; Ramachandran; Mr TP Vinayaka Rao; Prof KS Kannan; N Srinivasa Murthy; Mr Petit-Pierre Bugnion; Rasa Sha; Sister Brigit-Carol; Raven Silverwing; Lynna Dhanani; The Bead Museum, Glendale, Arizona; the estate of Paula Giese. Thanks, finally, to all at Carroll and Brown, especially Anna Amari-Parker for her dedication to and enthusiasm for the subject.

Credits for quotations:

Rabbi Yerachmiel Askotzky, p48; Sri Swami Sivananda, p67; Reverend Ido Miyahara and Craig Bratcher, p79; Waliullah al-Dahlawi from Dr Muhammad Hamidullah's *Introduction to Islam*, p89; Noorallah G. Juma and www.salmanspiritual.com and *The Name and the Named* (Fons Vitae) by Shaykh Tosun Bayrak, pp92–93; Black Elk from Michael Fitzgerald's *Yellowtail: Crow Medicine Man and Sun Dance Chief*, (University of Oklahoma Press), p101. Every effort has been made to obtain permission to reproduce the copyright material. The publishers and authors apologise for any omissions, which are wholly unintentional, and will make any necessary corrections in future editions of this book.

Where to buy prayer beads, ropes and threads:

Catholic rosaries: www.rosaryworkshop.com; www.rosaryshop.com
Orthodox rosaries: www.home.earthlink.net/~haywoodm/PrayerBeads.html
Anglican and Episcopalian rosaries: www.solitariesofdekoven@juno.com; www.home.earthlink.net/~haywoodm/PrayerBeads.html
Celtic rosaries: www.celtic-rosary.com
Tefillin: www.STAM.net
Buddhist and Hindu *malas:* www.khandro.net; www.fourgates.com; www.tiger-tiger.com; www.rudraksha.co.uk
Tasbih: www.halalco.com
Native American beadwork: www.berrybeadwork.com; www.Antiques–Internet.com; www.ancientwayswest.com
Worry beads: www.worryknot.com; www.komboloi.gr
Power beads: www.sacredgems.com
Goddess beads: www.CindyCraigStudios.com

Photographic credits:

Jacket: (front) Gray Henry; (back, top left) Lawrence Manning/Corbis; (back, top right) Gray Henry/Brynn Bruijn/Aramco World; (back, bottom) Gray Henry; **1** Richard L'Anson/Lonely Planet Images (LPI); **2** Gray Henry/Sultan Ghalib al-Quaiti; **8–9** World Religions Photolibrary; **11** The Art Archive (AA)/Museo di Castelvecchio Verona/Dagli Orti; **13** Paul Quenon@The Monastery of Gethsemane; **14** Chris Mellor/LPI; **16–17** Richard L'Anson/LPI; **18–19** Paul A Souders/Corbis; **21** Gray Henry; **24** AA/Galleria Brera Milan/Dagli Orti (A); **32–35** Gilda Pacitti; **36** Paul A Souders/Corbis; **43** World Religions Photolibrary; **44** Getty Images; **46–47** Paul Doyle/LPI; **49** E & E Picture Library/S Kahlon; **51** AA/Israel Museum Jerusalem/Dagli Orti; **52** David Tumley/Corbis; **55** Ted Spiegel/Corbis; **58–59** Lawrence Manning/Corbis; **61** Richard L'Anson/LPI; **65** Sara-Jane Cleland/LPI; **72–75** Gray Henry; **76** Jules Selmes; **77–80** Gray Henry; **81** Cheryl Conlon/LPI; **83** Gray Henry; **84** Jules Selmes; **86–87** Dave Bartruff/Corbis; **88** Gray Henry; **89** Gray Henry/Sultan Ghalib al-Quaiti; **90** Gray Henry; **91** Gray Henry/Brynn Bruijn/Aramco World; **94** Gray Henry/Chester Beatty Collection; **95** Hans Georg Roth/Corbis; **98–99** Lois Ellen Frank/Corbis; **103** David Peevers/LPI; **104–105** Grant Smith/Corbis; **109** Mic Looby/LPI.